BECOMING

WHO

YOU'RE

MEANT

TO BE

Eliminate destructive patterns and unlock the ultimate you.

KIMBERLY LOU

Becoming Who You're Meant to Be. © 2019 Kimberly Lou

KLC Publishing
ISBN: 9781686422461 - Paperback

Printed in the U.S.A.
First Edition, 2019

Cover photo: Brystan Studios, CA.
Cover design: Album Agency - www.albumagency.com

A lot of the ideas and concepts I am excited to share with you are derived from my own personal experience. Experience as an integrative life mentor and a long history of success! Please do as I did and consult an MD or PHD for authority on any matters of mental health, diet and exercise programs.

CONTENTS

FOREWORD

As a Board Certified Psychiatrist, I treat patients every day suffering from mental illness. I can attest, first hand, to the reality of an ever-increasing patient population of folks who are burned out, over extended and exhausted with life. Inundated with pressures every day, from everywhere to do more, be more, and give more – this is ever present and constant in the social media driven technology age we live in. According to the Centers for Disease Control 50% of all Americans will be diagnosed with a mental illness at some point in their life. Anxiety is the #1 mental health diagnosis with approximately 40 million people in the US suffering from an anxiety disorder.

These statistics have increased over the past decade and show no sign of slowing down. A proactive approach to mitigate rising anxiety in younger and younger ages needs to be addressed. Kimberly Lou is on the right track in this book giving people a way to potentially prevent debilitating mental illnesses in their lives.

My first impression upon meeting Kimberly Lou, who had just moved in next door with her preschool aged daughter, was that she was a very outgoing, dynamic person. As our families became better acquainted her clear moral compass, strong work ethic and desire to help others as a fitness professional & life coach, was evident. A few years after first meeting and learning her whole story, including her road to recovery, she became a part of the team utilized for groups with my patients in residential mental health and addiction treatment. Her unique coaching approach was well received, motivating and a great compliment to the treatment team.

I have personally seen the benefit to my patients working with Kimberly Lou. She is able to provide tangible tools and resources for people to utilize throughout their lives to maximize their success and happiness. In this book is a comprehensive approach to living the best life possible for you while getting the most out of every day. Becoming More covers the areas of life that everyone struggles to balance in this super paced world and gives you the instructions for overcoming obstacles that keep you down, robbing individuals of their energy and strength. I encourage everyone to read on to learn from someone who has been able to build herself up against incredible odds; someone who has always strived to become more.

Richard Granese, M.D., MBA

FOREWORD

Many see these times as the absolute best times in the history of our beautiful planet. Especially here in the United States!! Our declaration of independence states that we endowed with unalienable rights including life, liberty and the pursuit of happiness. This sounds great on paper and it is a beautiful standard. However, very few people are enjoying these freedoms.

Many people suffer the bondage of ill health. As one of my mentors' states "It's hard for a man to change the world when he has a hard time getting out of bed!" Fortunately for you, Kimberly Lou is a master at enhancing human energy and fitness. One of her super powers is finding ways to make fitness fun so that you can enjoy the entire journey. Every day and in every way, you can look forward to getting better and better!

Emotional Freedom may almost seem paradoxical. We are free to choose all of our emotions all of the time. However, when we choose subconsciously, we can become slaves to our emotions. Do you personally have, or do you have any friends who have consistent patterns of unserving emotions? I have never met anyone who has mastered this freedom every moment of every day. That great news is that Kimberly has outlined proven strategies to both get to the root of the emotions and to resolve these emotions fast.

The final component of your transformation to personal freedom is Mindset. Kimberly will guide you through an exercise where you unpack your Belief System (BS). And for most of us, it is our BS that keeps us locked into circumstances that keep us from being our best selves. Once your BS is unpacked Kimberly will walk you through time proven techniques to leave your limiting BS behind you.

Enjoy this fun read and most of all, enjoy your Personal Freedom!!!

Dr Bob Rakowski, DC, CCN, DACBN, DIBAK

TESTIMONIALS

When I met Kimberly, I knew she was someone special. I quickly felt her energy and her "want" to help others. In this book, she eloquently takes the mind/body connection to another level. My only suggestion is that you make a decision to get out of your head and into your heart when reading and apply the principles ASAP. You won't be disappointed.

Brian Bradley - The Egoscue Method – Tony Robbins Company – NFL

If you really want to learn practical down-to-earth skills for upgrading your life, read this book. Kimberly Lou touches on not only how to change your life but what has been holding you back from being your best self. She teaches life improving skills through her own experience, strength and hope. She knows what works because she has been where you are now. She will lead you to your optimal self through her own experiences.

"When I started my journey, I was completely imbalanced, weighing close to 200 pounds, smoking two packs of cigarettes each day, and I had neither a plan nor income." There is no better teacher than one who has already overcome the adversity that is holding you back. You can trust that she has experienced the pain and difficulty that you are in and knows the best steps for moving out of it.

If you need an upbeat, positive, and motivating book, this is the one for you. This book will travel with you on your destiny to greatness. Read it from cover to cover and then begin watching all of your dreams come true.

DeAnna Jordan Crosby, AMFT, LAADC
Clinical Director - New Method Wellness

BECOMING

WHO

YOU'RE

MEANT

TO BE

INTRODUCTION

What gives some people the ability to take their lives to heightened levels of success while others can barely make it through the day? How can we become the person we know deep down we were meant to be without burning out or breaking down? Many of you are already successful, but it seems like it's impossible to reach your greatest potential because you feel you are already operating at your maximum capacity.

What if I were to tell you that there is a source so great and so powerful within you that all you need to do is tap into it? I am here to tell you there is a whole other level of success you never even knew existed. Imagine a great source that is enormously rewarding, yet all it takes to access this source is a change of your old ideas.

In my program, I will teach you how to build a solid foundation for your new life using your personal freedom as your foundation. Now, this new book is titled *Becoming Who You're Meant to Be,* and it is about reaching your full potential. I am writing this book from my experience, and it is based on techniques I have developed and used myself.

Let me tell you a little about me. I was at the pinnacle of my career. My business was thriving, my social and home life was a happy one, and yet I didn't have the energy to sustain my schedule. I remember telling a friend I needed to slow down. She said, "Kim, you don't need to slow down. You just need to become more." Later, as I sat in meditation, I asked myself, what does "become more" mean? I wanted to understand this:

"Why do we become so burdened and burned out from life?" And then it hit me: "Because we are trying to tap into the wrong source. We are drawing on unhealthy beliefs that cause us to want to try to make things "happen" or that encourage us to "push through" the pain.

Yes, we do want to move through the pain, but not push. Pushing comes with major resistance. What I realized was that no matter how much success I had, it came with a price—my energy and vitality. My clients are no different. I've often heard, "Kim, I don't know how," or "I can't sustain my big life. I can't keep up." When I hear those words, "I don't know how," or, "I can't," I hear the subtext behind them: *"I don't want to."* They don't want to deal with the hassle or the extra work they believe it's going to take to change.

Let me tell you this program is not about *doing* more. I am going to show you secrets that will allow you to tap into inner resources you never knew you had, so you can become more, too! You will learn to let go of the struggle of "Making it Happen" and allow your life to bloom through you. I will teach you how to unlearn old habits and belief systems and ask yourself constant daily questions like: What do I want from my life? What must I let go of? And most importantly: Who must I become? You will learn to plant seeds and sustain your big beautiful life; you will enhance it and grow it!

There Is a Solution

The answer deals with conserving essential energy and preserving your precious vitality. In this book, *Becoming Who You're Meant to Be*, we discover the things one must do to conserve energy. Not only will you learn to take your life, your business, and your health to the next level, I also will teach you how to sustain it and become more. Each section of this book will take you through scientifically proven strategies to apply in your daily life to take your life to the next level.

But like any video game, every time you take your life, your business—or anything for that matter—to the next level, there will always be a breakdown. Often, each time we hit a milestone and think life is going to get easier, quite the opposite happens and it becomes more complicated.

And it is true. When you begin to take your life to the next level, more will be thrown at you. You will go through growing pains and, at times, it will feel like, "what the fuck am I even doing this for?" However, if you integrate my techniques, I will show you that just around the corner there is a source of untapped potential you didn't know was there. And not just a little potential; you will be able to fall in love with your life again, leave the stress of work at work, and create the loving family that has your back all over again. I will teach you how to "10X" your potential and harness your energy so you can become more.

Stand Up!

What if I told you life was a mental game, and that I didn't achieve a successful, well-adjusted life by using money, fame, or education? I didn't attract it with looks, with confidence, or anyone helping me. What if I told you that everything you want to accomplish is inside of you right now? Even if you don't currently have access to the tools you'll need, they can be easily accessed.

Whether they're training for the body they want, seeking the energy to sustain a big lifestyle, or trying to find emotional balance and the feeling of being happy, everybody can overcome self-imposed limitations. Ask me how I know! Not only have I done this for myself, I have helped thousands to achieve big results. That being said, I personally tried almost every kind of workout program and diet regimen, and I've ingested every supplement you can imagine. In addition, I acquired over 200 certifications while searching to find the simplest way to connect mind and body in order to deal with my own struggles.

When I started my journey, I was completely imbalanced, weighing close to 200 pounds, smoking two packs of cigarettes each day, and I had neither a plan nor income. I had a seventh-grade education, and I had just left my husband of ten years. Furthermore, my career of 16 years had come crashing to a halt. To say I was at the lowest of the low was an understatement: I was sleeping on a friend's floor trying to figure out what I wanted to do with my life. I had lost my sense of purpose, my energy, and all hope. As a result, I turned to my usual support systems in the form of drugs, alcohol, and bingeing and purging six times a day. I was an emotional wreck chained to my addictions, my negative mindset, and my victim consciousness. Each time I tried to make a change, I would quickly burn out and quit because my lifestyle and plan were unsustainable.

These days, my life is more than a little different. I just got back from an amazing two-week trip to London with my beautiful daughter. Instead of living in my car, I'm now living in my dream home and driving a new luxury SUV. I'm in the best shape of my life. In addition, as an Integrative Mentor who coaches High Achievers, I have been featured on many media platforms, landed a spot on a number-one-ranked radio show, and have appeared on E! Entertainment, MTV, HBO, ESPN, MSNBC, and ShowTime.

I also created a successful online empire as an Advanced Fitness and Wellness Specialist, helping people achieve Emotional Fitness. My clients include billion-dollar CEO's and their executive teams. I've coached professional athletes who have gone from suffering constant pain, injuries, and an "I can't do it" attitude to being top-ranked in their field. I did this by helping them achieve the mindset needed to catapult them to success. I've trained Olympic athletes who were experiencing emotional turmoil due to relationships that almost took them out of the game; by helping them manage their emotions, they ultimately achieved the gold medal. I've helped A-list celebrities deal with insecurities in a feast-or-famine industry. I've helped CEOs manage the emotional stress of having to employ, take care of, and provide payroll for thousands of employees. I've helped business owners quadruple their incomes in less than 90 days by guiding them to manage emotions such as anxiety, stress, fear, doubt, worry, and even anger for having so much responsibility on their plate. In other arenas, I have worked with families dealing with major addictions and mental illnesses like schizophrenia and dissociative identity disorders, helping them create blueprints for lives they came to love.

What all my clients had in common was that it took emotional fitness to help them manage their energy. I'm talking about the kind of life-sustaining energy that propels us to our purpose and ultimately helps us live the life of our dreams. Outwardly these people appeared successful, but inwardly they struggled with emotional pain that held them back.

So how did I go from someone living in their car—living in desperation with no income, no purpose, and no education—to someone successfully helping so many others? I did it through managing my big emotions, my energy, and my mindset. Using the tools I describe in this book, I learned what triggers my big emotions, and I learned to manage my stress. I also realized that the reason I wasn't moving forward in my life was because I only knew how to live the old way. I had no clue how to live a new, expansive, and amazing life. I didn't have the tools, and I couldn't visualize success because I didn't know that kind of life could exist for me. I only knew how to think about what was familiar to me, which meant being in scarcity and in survival mode.

When I allowed myself to daydream about what I wanted, even though it seemed impossible, that desire ultimately motivated me to take action. Also, I began to ask people who had achieved great success what they had done so that I could mimic them. I read hundreds of self-help books and my career began to grow. However, I still had those big, negative emotions that threatened to take me out of the game of life.

I learned through trial and error what worked to minimize my stress when facing major change and, ultimately, the anxiety went away. I didn't say my fear went away, but my anxiety did. Fear (Face Everything And Recover) was the major motivator for my success. The fear of not succeeding was so much greater because I knew that, if I didn't change, I would suffer from those big emotions for the rest of my life. The thought of suffering was much more painful than taking the uncomfortable risks necessary to create a new, exciting adventure for my life.

The question you may have going through your mind right now may be: "Is it possible for anyone to do this?" The answer is a resounding "Yes!" I have worked with the deeply challenged people who were dealing with drug addiction and mental illnesses such as schizophrenia and dissociative identity disorder, and I have seen with my own eyes how miracles can and will take place as a result of following my program. I have seen people transform right before my eyes, whether rich or poor, perfectly sane or mentally ill.

If I can change so can you. All you need is the willingness to do the work. I have done the heavy lifting for you. Anyone can follow this program and change for the better. Most people are afraid to start a new program because they are afraid it is going to be hard or think it will take hours upon hours every day. This program has done all the groundwork for you. All you need to do is read a chapter each week and take the simple steps each day to move into your new life. I didn't win the lottery. Nobody saved me. I wasn't merely lucky. I simply planted small seeds for 15 minutes each morning, added exercise into my day, and ate foods that fueled my body perfectly. Those small adjustments each day accumulated to create a whole new healthy lifestyle.

My Stand Up Story

During the summer of 1988, I spent most of my days going to the beach. I was a beach girl, even though it took me over two hours each way by bus to get there. I didn't care. The pleasure I experienced when I arrived was worth the four-hour ride. The beach was one place where I felt free, splashing around in the waves. The sun beaming on my skin and the smell of suntan lotion was euphoric (coconut... hmmm). I was 14.

The waves on this particular day were four feet or more. I couldn't wait to dive into the water. I could hear the seagulls and the waves crashing. The wind was blowing just enough to cool the beams of sun on my skin. It was a perfect summer's day. As I ran to the water, leaving a trail of clothes behind me, I knew my personal freedom was merely moments away. My body hit the water, and I felt the cool of the ocean on my skin. It was refreshing. I splashed, I played, and then I felt something take me under the water. As I battled to swim my way to the top to gasp for air, a wave came crashing down, pushing me down again to the bottom of the ocean. I struggled to swim to the top. Yet another wave pushed and then pulled me to the bottom. I came to the conclusion that I was going to die. I knew I would! Looking back, I had no idea that this was going to be a sign of things to come, a way of living that was going to take me out if I didn't do anything about it. As I struggled to the surface, a lifeguard began to run my way. Maybe, just maybe, I was going to make it. *Maybe he will save me*, I thought. Then he stopped; the lifeguard who was supposed to save me stopped! Why wasn't he running into the water to pull me out? What the hell was wrong with him? He just stood there, shouting. As if I could hear. *Why the hell is he not saving me?* I thought. I was clearly drowning.

This seemed to be the story of my life: abandoned. Once again, I was left alone, nobody cared for me. I epitomized the victim. Why didn't anybody love me enough to save me? The lifeguard yelled again, but I couldn't hear because another wave came crashing down on my body like a ten-ton elephant. Again, I scraped the bottom of the sea floor and, once again, I swam back up and strained to hear him saying something else.

I screamed in anger and sheer panic, "Save me!"

He shouted again. Clearly, this man saw me struggling! Why wasn't he helping me?

Tears streaming down my face, I shouted, "Please save me!" Once again, he yelled. This time I heard him. "Stand up!"

"Stand up?" I shouted, "How?"

"Just put your feet down onto the ground and stand up."

I did what I was directed to do. To my amazement, my feet planted firmly onto the sand. Apparently, I had been drowning in two feet of water! Ashamed, embarrassed, (hey, that lifeguard was super cute), and exhausted from my experience, I picked up my shattered ego and crawled onto my towel where I lay sobbing. That was going to be symbolic for many of my life experiences to come. Many times, I allowed my emotions to overtake me, so much so that it caused illness to the point of being diagnosed with PTSD. If I knew then what I know now—that I did have the ability to save myself—I would have been able to salvage my broken marriage, I would have had the self-worth to obtain the job of my dreams, and I could have recovered my health without creating the stress-induced auto-immune disorder that was robbing me of my serenity. Looking back now, there are parts of me that are grateful that I was able to experience and overcome all of these things. However, I needlessly suffered, and I didn't want to drown in my emotions any longer. It was time for a change.

It has been said that everything happens for a reason. In my case, I think it was so I could pass my life lessons on to you. And yet, how sweet would it have been if I'd had someone like the new me to give the old me tools to avoid all that grief. I don't want anyone else to go through what I went through and suffer unnecessarily. So, if you are sick and tired of being sick and tired and of being ruled by your emotions, or if your life hasn't kicked your ass yet but you know it will if you don't make some life-altering changes, then stay tuned. This book details my personal Hero's Journey toward healing, as well as offering a step-by-step guide to help you do the same.

And I'm still not done "standing up." I have bigger plans, and I want to help more people. I've found my purpose, and that purpose is compelling me to write this book, to launch my video series on YouTube and Social Media, to create free content online, and to teach workshops, hold seminars and do so much more!

First, join me in this mental exercise. I want you to picture where you are right now. Are you where you want to be in your life or do you want more? Think about that. Next, I want you to imagine living the life that you love. What are you doing? Where are you going? How are people responding to you? Now, allow yourself to daydream. In your dream, do you have abundant energy? Are you excited about life?

Paint this new picture of how you want your life to be in each of these areas:
- Health and Fitness
- Relationships
- Business
- Spirituality

My goal is to help you live a more vital, healthy and happy life. I want you to FALL IN LOVE with yourself and your life. This is a whole new journey we are going to take, and guess what? You don't have to do it alone! We are going to work it out together! I am going to show you what I did for myself and for thousands of others. Whether you want to lose weight or make better lifestyle choices, I can help you get there in half the time.

It wasn't until I stopped trying to force myself to make huge changes all at once that I was able to develop new patterns. By adding simple, small steps, I replaced my negative habits with healthy positive changes one little step at a time. And it didn't happen overnight. Because of my past painful experiences, I ultimately achieved Emotional Fitness. I have designed this 90-Day *Becoming Who You're Meant to Be* Program to help you "Stand Up" and live the life you have always wanted, because....YOU CAN!

Get ready for a new life-changing adventure that is also fun!

Kimberly Lou

CHAPTER I
Becoming Who You're Meant to Be

"The energy of the mind is the essence of life."
—Aristotle

If you are reading this book, chances are you desire something more for your life. Perhaps it's a beautiful body, a healthy lifestyle, and a peaceful soul: something *more*. Am I right? That's exactly what I wanted, too, although I felt stuck, afraid, and hopeless.

Physical Pain

As a single mother, I worked 60-70 hours per week with over 40 clients to mentor. As a result of my demanding schedule and fast-paced lifestyle, I developed ulcers, gastritis, and an unidentified autoimmune disorder that took over my body. I was in chronic pain. Every time I ate food, even healthy food, my body would develop burning internal pain all over. My physical energy was depleted, and inflammation was increasing in my body. I knew that if I didn't make a change, I was going to crash, and crash fast. So, what did I do? I resorted to my old patterns of trying to survive.

Emotional Survival

Unconsciously, I activated defenses to cope with my pain. When we find ourselves in a life-or-death situation, defenses cause the body to react with either a fight, flight, or freeze mode. The problem is that these emotional survival skills are not required in everyday life. With prolonged use, they cause you to cope in ways that are not helpful. For example, I couldn't stop drinking to save my life, and I overate to cope with the pressure. I isolated myself from supportive friends. Fear overcame me as I tried, with little success, to fall asleep. Confusion consumed me. I simply didn't know how to change my habits. I didn't know how to live my life differently. On a deeper level, I wasn't comfortable experiencing goodness in my life because I didn't think I deserved it. The truth is, I felt comfortable with my defenses. They were the very habits that had helped comfort me and regulated my emotions through hard times. At the end of a hard day, a glass—or bottle—of wine took away my stress. That box of chocolate comforted my soul. The next day when I woke up, riddled with regret, I quickly realized my emotional survival skills had failed me again. They failed my ailing body with weight gain and more hopelessness.

Maybe you can relate? Do you have emotional survival skills you use to cope with crises or to protect yourself during a difficult time? Are those same emotional survival skills now killing you? Your old survival skills will no longer work for you when you are doing any or all of the following:

- working long hours with no sleep,
- drinking tons of caffeine to keep you awake
- pushing past your physical threshold when your body is screaming for you to stop.

Some call this burning the candle at both ends. Western culture expects us to live at this pace with no rest. However, if you continue at this pace, those survival skills that once worked for you will ultimately kill you. Prolonged use of unhealthy emotional survival skills will cause anxiety, mental illness, depression, addiction, chronic illness, diabetes, autoimmune disorders, bowel disorders, thyroid and adrenal disorders, skin rashes, canker sores, cancer, heart disease and even death. You ask me how I know this? Read on.

Finding Hope

With the weight of the world on my shoulders, I knew if I continued to live that way, I would collapse. In agonizing fear, it was time to face my mortality. Was I going to die? What if my illness got so bad, I couldn't work? Who was going to take care of my daughter if something happened to me? These questions became a constant parade through my brain. At night, I cried myself to sleep because I didn't know what to do. One night the fear was so great, I got down on my knees and begged God to give me the willingness and the knowledge to change. I remember telling a friend that my life had gotten too big and I needed to slow down. Worst of all, I felt crazy. I didn't have any time for myself, much less the energy to take care of my child. I had lost my zest. I used to be so much fun, but now I was burned out, in pain, and my life was messy. I wanted to enjoy life; the trouble was I didn't even know how to have fun anymore. I had hit rock bottom.

Finding Answers

I believe God sends angels at just the right time, and this time, the message coming from my friend was the most profound yet simple thing I had ever heard. She said: "My beautiful friend, life can be fun, and you can do it. You don't have to slow down. You just need to become more."

"What does that mean?" I asked.

Her initial words made me envision twenty clowns trying to squeeze their way into a VW Bug. Did she expect me to fit more things into my over-scheduled life?

I replied, slightly annoyed, "Clearly you didn't hear me. I don't have extra time *to become more.*"

She said, "Lovely lady, I didn't say pack more into your day. I said, '*Become more!*'"

"I have no idea what you mean," I told her.

She said, "You're a smart girl. Meditate on the statement '*become more*' and figure it out."

Later, as I sat in meditation, I asked myself, "What does it mean, to '*become more?*'"

Who would I have to be "*to become more*"? What would I have to do? What skills and tools would I need to acquire in order to have a better quality of life? How much time was it going to take to learn "*to become more*"?

> "*The higher your energy level, the more efficient your body. The more efficient your body, the better you feel and the more you will use your talent to produce outstanding results.*"
> —Anthony Robbins

Then, the thought came to me: It's not about time management, it's about energy management. Learn to harness your energy, redirect it, and put it into your projects. Hmmm, Energy Management! I realized there was a way to become more emotionally fit—a way to become more by redirecting my emotional energy into productive lifestyle changes. As I understood more about emotional fitness, I realized I could become more of a whole person. Now, how could I do that?

Start with Meditation

Every day, I sat quietly and meditated for fifteen minutes on how to manage my emotional energy more efficiently. I spent every waking hour reading books and listening to Audible recordings. I was hungry for answers about how to emotionally regulate. Ultimately, the answers began to pour out of me, and I began to share my newfound knowledge with my clients.

I had trainers tell me that nobody would ever train with me under my new methodology. However, by combining emotional fitness into my teaching, my clients began to do half the training with twice the results, and within seven weeks, I was the top trainer at my gym. Not only that, I began to attract the attention of professional athletes, A-list celebrities, and CEO's of multi-billion-dollar corporations. Even doctors wanted me to help them conduct classes for the patients with mental illnesses and cognitive disorders.

What all these clients had in common was they were burned out from life, exactly as I had been! Not only did I have the answers they were looking for, I had actually been through the same thing: I could completely relate to them. I could give them hope because there was an answer for them. They could do it. It was going to be okay. And my promise to you, if you do what is suggested in this program, is that you, too, will be okay! You will become more vibrant. You will be able to harness your energy and find your motivation. In addition, this program will help you to restore your health, lose weight, and yes, *"become more"*!

My *Becoming Who You're Meant to Be* Program is a 12-week, step-by-step guide to help you shift your mindset around mental, emotional, and physical fitness, creating a mind/body connection and harnessing sustainable energy. Why? Because everything starts with your mental fitness which contributes to supporting your central nervous system. When you have negative thoughts, they tear down your body. There is a mind/body connection: you can't heal one without healing the other.

However, there needs to be a shift to create that sustainable energy.

> *"The energy you bring, positive or negative, dictates your*
> *perceptions, receptions, and radiations."*
> —T.F. Hodge

All this is to say: how is your life working for you now? Is it time for a change? If the answer is yes, then keep reading. This book will guide you step-by-step. I have done all the research for you. All you need to do is show up, roll up your sleeves, and make the small sustainable changes each week for 12 weeks—12 short weeks for a whole new mindset and lifestyle shift. The goal is to help you move out of survival mode and into thriving mode. Have you been living a certain way that worked for you at one time, but it no longer does? If so, your unconscious mind will resist change because your old habits have become comfortable to you. That's why I prefer to add new behaviors one week at a time. This is a lifestyle shift, and if I recommended that you change everything at once, I would be setting you up for failure.

Studies have shown it takes 40 days to release an old habit and 90 days to replace that habit with a new one, meaning this is not a quick fix. If that's what you're looking for, this program is not for you. This is a mindset shift designed to create a lifestyle and body built to last. Also remember, chances are quick fixes haven't worked for you in the past, or you wouldn't be reading this book. How will this work? Here is the roadmap: in this book, we will go over a three-pronged approach to Emotional Fitness.

- Mental Focus
- Emotional Fitness
- Physical Training

With Mental Focus Management, we tap into your Limited Belief System. We all have it, and our belief systems keep us stuck and running old programs in the background of our minds, wasting precious energy. It's like having many programs running on your computer at one time. Even though you can only see one, there are several others draining the battery. It's the same with your Mind/Body connection. The computer in your brain may be running multiple programs that drain your central nervous system, short-circuiting the motherboard to your brain, which in turn affects your entire body's function and system.

Physical Training will give you the vehicle to skyrocket your body in order to sustain your journey. That doesn't mean you have to kill yourself or pay hundreds of dollars in gym fees. I'm here to tell you: I've been without gyms before, and I worked out at home. You can do the same in your own home very simply. I will show you how. In the Physical Training section, I will teach you how to use your body as a vehicle to keep up with the demands of your life. You can either be a rocket ship or a broken-down car. Since I can't get you to the moon in a crummy, seen-better-days, broken-down vehicle, you'll need to choose.

With mental and emotional fitness, you will use visualization techniques to obtain clarity on what you want and why you want it. You will also learn how to tap into a constant stream of ideas and beliefs that will help you fulfill your life's purpose. Many programs offer to help you set goals. However, if you don't have a purpose behind those goals, your healthy changes may not last. I ask my gym clients what they want. Most often, their goal is, "I want to look great naked." That is a great goal and, yes, you will achieve that through this program. However, it is your purpose—and the "why" behind your purpose—that will help drive that goal home and will result in lasting change for the better.

Knowing your purpose and the why behind your purpose is the key to helping you harness your goal and achieve it. Beyond that, your new self-knowledge will help you discover a higher purpose, one that will drive you toward enjoying the vision/ process. THAT VISION IS SUPER IMPORTANT! Once we have that vision, we will begin to plant seeds in your unconscious mind by using meditation and visualization to connect you with your best, happiest, healthiest life.

Here are the steps we'll take to achieve your new amazing life:

1. Identifying and Unpacking Limiting Belief Systems: If it's hysterical, it's historical.
2. Adrenal Fatigue: Creating Sustainable Energy
3. Universal Language of Energy: Energy Management
4. Harness, Enhance, and Elevate Your Energy
5. Purpose Mindset
6. Tap Into Resources You Never Knew You Had
7. Mental Imagery
8. Making Your Rocket Fuel
9. Body Transformation Made Easy
10. Pay It Forward: We can't keep what we have unless we give it away.
11. Achieve Results
12. Planning

There's no membership required, no initiation fees. This is my love project to you. There are many people suffering out there. I am here to say that, not only have I overcome these difficulties, I am thriving and you can, too! My promise to you is if you do what is suggested in this program, you will become more vibrant, you will learn to harness your energy, and you will find motivation. This program will help you restore your health and become more mentally, emotionally, and physically fit. This book will teach you how to lighten up and smile more while rolling with the punches of your fast-paced lifestyle. I have completed all the research for you and have successfully trained over 10,000 people in my new methodology with sustainable results!

Becoming Who You're Meant to Be is a simple a step-by-step blueprint which will give you the tools to achieve your desired results. Keep this in mind: simple not easy. This program requires a mindset shift, and at first, your defenses will fight you. However, with my help each week, I will guide you to your new amazing life. What is there to lose? The program is free, and I can easily refund your misery, if you want to go back to your previous lifestyle. However, if you want sustainable change, let's roll up our sleeves together!

CHAPTER II
Is No One Safe From the BS (Belief Systems)?

We all know life can be hard, and if you're reading this book you are probably not where you want to be. You might be wondering, "Why is this happening to me? Why am I stuck? Why don't I have the success that my peers do? How come my body is reacting in the way it is? I don't feel as vibrant and energetic as I used to." Questions like these can keep you spinning your wheels, going nowhere fast. The reason is your Belief System. In a previous chapter, I explained my false belief that I was drowning in deep water; my false belief was killing me! The truth was that I just needed to put my feet down because the water was only two feet deep! As silly as my Stand Up story seems, it illustrates perfectly how all of my self-imposed stories, and the significance I added to them, created a world full of needless suffering.

"Pain is inevitable but suffering is optional...you choose."
–Viktor Frankl

The suffering you experience in life is very often a result of your Belief System, your BS, the story you choose to tell yourself. This story can result in massive suffering that you carry with you like a huge sack of rocks throughout your whole life. You may want to escape the suffering and achieve your dreams, but you may not have the tools. Even if you know where you want to go in life and how you want your life to be, you first need the tools to lose that sack of rocks and escape your suffering.

I was talking with a friend the other day while watching people outside the window enjoying the pool and the sun. It was a beautiful day. While talking, we noticed a fly. The fly was trying with all of its might to push through the window to escape outside. It pushed and pushed and pushed, continuously banging his head against the glass to no avail. He knew where he wanted to go, but he couldn't achieve it no matter how much he struggled. It reminded me of the saying, "If people could do better, they would." However, many do not have the knowledge or the tools to achieve their goals. That poor fly! If only he knew that all he had to do was change direction and discover the nearby open door. There, he would find peace, but he gave up exhausted from spinning his wheels and going nowhere fast. Many of us do the very same thing.

Not only has this same misdirection happened in my life, but I've also noticed the same occurrence with my clients over the past 15 years. I have seen much needless suffering, and I guarantee that if you learn to change your BS, you'll look back at what you used to believe and find it is just as ridiculous. And it will no longer have any power over you.

Before I can help you become ready for your success, we need to address what's happening to you right now. It begins with your Belief System. What I have discovered is that we need to address your Belief System before we can delve into this program. If we're not careful, your Belief System, which I call BS—literally, your bullshit—can and will take you out of the game of life.

A Belief System is your personal story that you tell yourself every day, day in and day out. We are taught our BS growing up, and through our successes, tragedies, and especially our failures, we are creating a thought system that shapes our actions. It affects everything we do. Everything! I often say to clients, "If it's hysterical, it's historical." This classic expression from the recovery movement says it all. In other words, when I am "triggered," dealing with big emotions like stress, anxiety, fear, doubt, anger, worry, and being overwhelmed, these feelings are coming from a past trauma. Inevitably, if I find myself becoming overly emotional, there is a reason for it, and it usually stems from a past trauma.

Suzy.

Suzy was a client of mine. I was training her one day, and she expressed how she could never get a second date. Her excuse was that men were shallow and didn't like her because she was heavy. I disagreed. I said, "If they had a problem with your weight, why would they have asked you out in the first place. It has nothing to do with your weight and everything to do with the energy you are putting out."

She fought me on this concept for a while until she began to see a pattern. When she realized that I might be on to something, she agreed to let me set her up on a blind date. I went with her and a group of people to a restaurant. Within five minutes of her date's arrival, her behavior started to change. Once she felt he was attracted to her, her body language closed off, and she began to frown when she spoke to him. She acted as if she were competing with him, and she explained at length how hard she worked and what a strong woman she was. She made it very clear through her words and her body language that she was not available, and that there was no room in her life for him, let alone an ability for him to ever be the man in the relationship.

Suzy had no idea she was turning men off, but at an unconscious level, she used her weight and body language to protect herself from men, especially since she had been abused as a child by her father. When I asked her what she thought about men, she replied, "Men are pigs and can't be trusted." She had concluded, based on the experience she'd had with her father, that all men were like he was. As a result, she interacted with men as if none of them could be trusted. Again, if it's hysterical, which means you have a big emotion around something, then it's historical; it stems from a past memory, one from which you created a Belief System. As a result, Suzy's BS was, "All men are cheating, abusive pigs."

She created this BS as a result of the meaning she placed on the story of what had happened to her. She carried a preconceived notion that men were pigs, and she projected that with her body language and the energy she emitted. Men couldn't run from her fast enough. We had to change her BS around men and give her the tools to safely open up. When we did that, Suzy soon attracted her soul mate and, today, is happily married.

An example of BS among animals occurs with elephants at the circus. Most elephant trainers tie the animals up using steel bolts when they are babies. No matter how much the little elephant pulls, he can't break free. Then, when the elephant grows up, all the circus trainer has to do is tie the elephant with a string, and he won't try to escape. He has been programmed by his BS to stay put. I call this "Learned Helplessness." I have struggled with Learned Helplessness, big time. My "Stand Up" story demonstrates how I grew up thinking I was weak and a victim because, at one time, I was. I had no idea of the power and resiliency I had until I learned to set boundaries and clear my inner baggage. Oh, my life is so much freer now that I am not a victim. Thank God!

Now that you see how your own BS can trap you, let's do a little visualization. Pick an area in your life where you feel you have a loss of power. I call this a blind spot. This is going to help you identify where you need to spend your time in the next chapter uncovering and unpacking Your BS. But it starts with a question that will start the unpacking process. The question is this: What is the area in your life where you feel like you have the least power? It could be your health. For example, you may be overweight and have a hard time losing it. You could have low energy or even feel burned out. Maybe your loss of power is in your relationships, as with the story of my client above, or maybe you are not where to you want to be in your career. Whatever it is, write it down.

How do you feel when you think of this area of your life? Is this the first time this blind spot has come up, or is it a pattern which has developed over time? Remember, if it's hysterical, it's historical, meaning if something triggers you into a crazy state, it is usually based on a trauma that has happened in the past. For example, when someone says something or gives you a certain look, similar to the way your mom used to look at you when you were in trouble, it may trigger memories and feelings that go with that situation. When you think about this blind spot, do you feel light and fluffy, or do you feel heavy, burned out, stressed, or exhausted? Now, imagine carrying it with you for five years. How do you feel carrying the weight of the past on your shoulders? How's your energy? Next, carry this blind spot for ten years. How do you feel now? How much longer do you think your body will be able to hold up? Do you love your life, or are you just burned out? Chances are, you feel exhausted simply by thinking about this scenario.

Okay, shake that projected future off and be thankful that it hasn't happened.

Knowing that you have a choice and the power to change, let's play a different game: what if you didn't have the old BS? What if you could have whatever you wanted? Think about that old pattern being resolved. What does your energy feel like now? How about your health? People often have numerous self-imposed limitations, and they continue to fall back into the same patterns. Many clients say to me, "Yeah, well, the past does not equal the future." I say, "Hell yeah it does, if you continue to do the same things." Protecting your energy and your health is your most important contribution to the relationships around you. So, the question is, how are you going to change?

To further illustrate my point, I went to a website called *Leading Personality*. On the website is a popular, often-cited experiment, and what I can tell you is that I've seen this behavior in thousands of my clients. The story goes like this: A scientist placed a number of fleas in a glass jar. They quickly jumped out. He then put the fleas back into the jar and placed a glass lid over the top. The fleas began jumping and hitting the glass lid, falling back down into the jar. After a while, the fleas, conditioned to the presence of the glass lid, began jumping slightly below the glass lid so as not to hit it. The scientist then removed the glass lid, as it was no longer needed to keep the fleas in the jar. The fleas had learned to limit themselves from jumping beyond the height of the lid even when the lid was removed. They had been conditioned to the fact that they could not escape from the jar. Even their offspring did not try to jump past where the lid was.

Those who keep failing aren't failing because they can't do it; they have fooled themselves into believing that they can't. Most people do not want to change their old familiar habits even if the tools of change are attainable. They will continue to say they want success when, really, they are afraid of success and fear having to step up, face up and grow up. They would rather play the victim instead of accepting full responsibility for their lives. It seems many people would rather put their heads in the sand and pretend they don't know how to achieve what they want because, if they did, there would be no more playing small in what could become a big life. This quote from Marianne Williamson sums it up:

> *"Our deepest fear is not that we are inadequate. Our deepest fear is that we are powerful beyond measure."*
> —A Return to Love: Reflections on the Principles
> of A Course in Miracles

Some clients of mine say, "I have to argue with you there, Kim. I am not playing a small game. I have always been an over-achiever. Look at my house and my career. Most people would say that I am doing great work!" I say to them in return, "I get it. However, there is a big difference between achieving material means and then having the health and well-being to enjoy it. I understand you are playing a big game in life, yet the one area that matters—the area of healthy energy through mental, emotional, and physical fitness—usually takes a back burner. Why?"

Does the price of playing a big game in life mean the loss of well-being? For too many people, the big life means never-ending fight. Is the deer who is being chased by a pack of wolves going to stop and schedule a massage? Hell no! Is the deer, while he is being attacked, going to sit down and have a beautiful dinner and meaningful conversation with his beloved family? Again, no! And humans are no different. They tend to be afraid to slow down for fear that they won't be able to regain momentum or that the competition will eat them alive. If the deer is being chased, all he can think about is the predator, where the exits are, and how much time it has to get to safety. Nothing else. All the deer can think about is survival.

How do we grow into this survival mode, where does it stem from, and most importantly, how can we change it? Many of my very successful clients usually had something happen to them in childhood where they needed to step up and assume responsibility, even though they didn't want to. Either a parent, caretaker, someone from a team in school, or another person they depended on didn't do their part, and that child concluded in his or her mind that they now had to take the leadership role. As a result, they adopted a survival mode, became hyper-alert, and were rarely able to turn it off. As they grew up, everything they had ever accomplished was because they were afraid that if they took a break, they wouldn't be able to start back up again. This fear kept them in a hyper-vigilant mode.

I call this fear a survival skill. A computer analogy for this would be when you have several programs open on your computer at once. You only see one program; however, there are several others draining your battery and your energy. Belief Systems operate the same way. They will drain you of your precious life energy and, if not addressed, will quickly take you out of the game of life. My goal is to help you move out of survival mode and into thriving mode. Ultimately, you'll take all of that kinetic energy, amplify it, and redirect it into the life that you love. That pretty much sums up my whole approach to your new life: slow down to go fast.

How to Solve the Problem

Belief Systems can be changed. This is what I do every day, all day long. This is what I have been helping thousands of my clients achieve for many years; helping them uncover their BS, find the beginning point it stems from, and then changing that BS into something that serves them and works in their favor. I always tell my clients, "Heck, if you're going to make up BS about yourself and create a story around it, it might as well be a good story, one that works to make your life better." Because what ever you say to yourself, you will believe.

What we all forget is that our thoughts are an illusion. They are not real. In my mind, I absolutely knew that I was drowning in my "stand up" story. And it's true, I was. However, it was only in two feet of water, and I was fully capable of putting my feet down, standing up, and saving myself. So, just stand up! How, you might ask? By making a shift in perspective. Have you ever heard of an accident taking place on a street corner and several witnesses giving several different stories of what happened? There are different perspectives. You are an expert witness to your life, and your job is to tell a better story, one that gets you motivated and excited, instead of one that disempowers you.

Exercise

- So, you have now identified where you have a loss of power in your life, and you have written it down. Ask yourself: what it is that makes you angry or upset about this?
- Next, write an angry letter to that person or situation that you are upset about. If anger is not the emotion, then express whatever it is that comes to you. Make sure you are explicit and express yourself fully in the letter.
- Once you are finished writing your letter, turn your paper over and draw the picture of how you see this situation. You can use a pencil, pen, or if you want to be more creative, use crayons. It doesn't have to be elaborate or perfect. It's there to help you experience the essence of your big emotion. You see, many people do not have the words to express themselves. This exercise assists you in expelling that big emotion, so you can let it out and ultimately let it go. Once you let it go, there is room for your new amazing life to fill that space.
- Once you have drawn a picture on the back of your letter, it's time to rip it up or burn it. You can also make a ritual out of disposing of this representation of your painful feelings. Whatever works for you.
- Lastly, on a new sheet of paper, draw the outcome you want to have happen in place of what has been happening. For example, if you are fighting with your spouse but you really want to experience a connection and love, then draw a picture of what you want your relationship to look like. That is going to plant a seed in your unconscious mind, saying, "This is what I want. Get to work and manifest that now."

I do this exercise often with my clients who have mental and cognitive disabilities. I also do this with my daughter, and it works wonders. You should see some of the angry letters she comes up with. She even drew one of her friends in jail. I had to stop myself from chuckling. As I mentioned, many people do not have the words to express what they are feeling. Therefore, they tend to unsuccessfully stuff those big emotion down. What happens then is that they blow up or create a neurotic behavior or fixation, like eating too much, drinking, or exhibiting some other unhealthy behavior to cover up that pain and as a way of compensating.

Now that you are mentally prepared and you have that pattern or blind spot firmly in your mind, we can begin the process of unpacking and changing your BS. I am super excited for you to get started!

CHAPTER III
Unpacking Your Beliefs

"Everyone comes with baggage. Find someone who loves you enough to help you unpack."

—Anonymous

Imagine this. I tell you I am going to take you on a journey, a trip if you will, and that we are going to see some amazing sights. All I want you to do is show up because I have everything covered. So, you arrive ready to go. I ask you to climb into the back seat of my car, stretch out your legs and relax. You comply and get settled in.

As you snuggle into the seat and make yourself comfortable, I jump into the back seat with you. You look puzzled and say, "Who's going to drive the car?"

I say, "Don't worry. I totally have this covered. I am going to have my 7-year-old daughter drive us to our destination."

If you were any sane person, you would say, "Are you frickin' kidding me? If we let your daughter drive, she will definitely crash and possibly kill us."

And yet as silly as this analogy is, many people allow their inner child, who is full of fears and old belief systems, to take the driver's seat in their lives. That child is very controlling and very loud. However, they are loud for a reason. He or she has been trying to get your attention for many years. We need to find a way to comfort that child so they can release their death grip on the steering wheel of life and let go of controlling the show. But how does one find the tools that enable that child to let go, so that you can buckle *them* safely into the back seat and give them a coloring book and crayons to occupy them for the journey?

Think of this chapter as a journey into your Self. On this journey, you are going to unpack and unlearn outdated Belief Systems so you can take control and enjoy the grand adventure into your new life. You are only allowed to bring eight articles for your trip. Why? Think about it. Everyone loves to travel, but baggage has become a major issue. If your bag is too big and stuffed with too many things, it can really cost you. It costs you time and money, physical labor, and emotional drain. Having the right baggage with just the right tools packed inside makes your travel a fun, freeing, and exciting new adventure.

Imagine that Emotional Fitness is a thrilling new journey for you, and that I am here as your personal unpacking assistant to help you keep what you need and let go of the rest. Let's get our feet wet in this 90-day program by introducing the eight items, the eight essential steps, that will help you "unpack your bags" and move into the life of your dreams. Let's meet the 8-Step Process!

In the last chapter, I introduced a saying that I love: "If it's hysterical, it's historical." I probably first heard it at a 12-Step meeting, and the saying stuck with me forever because it was so profound. Hysterical/Historical taught me that if I am blowing a situation way out of proportion, I need to look deeper. There is probably something going on from my past that is being triggered. These recurring patterns loom large and create powerful emotional states that take up far too much of our time and attention. When I look closely, I usually find that this is a repeated pattern that comes from childhood.

Why do we want to unpack your BS? I can't teach you a new approach to life with a mind full of BS. It won't work. I have to help you unpack and clear the clutter of your mind so you can see the truth. Because the truth can, and will, set you free. Once you are clear, then we can reprogram your mind with new beliefs. I need you clear! This process, which can seem daunting, usually takes no more than fifteen minutes, in many cases less. As we continue in the following chapters, I will also explain each step in further detail. To get started, I want to tell you a story which will help me illustrate how to clear your old BS step by step.

Step 1: Identifying the problem(s) you are dealing with now.

Danny.

Danny is the owner of a successful business. He came to me thinking he wanted to lose weight, but what he left with was so much more. In our first meeting, I could see Danny was burned out and exhausted from life. He had dark circles under his eyes, and his face was pale—a classic sign of adrenal fatigue. He mentioned that he had absolutely no energy, and he was overweight. Working with so many people in the past, I knew his concern went much deeper than just weight loss. He had a Belief System that was draining him of his precious energy. His physical condition wasn't the problem; it was an outcome of his BS. So, we had to figure out what his BS was because I knew that, if unaddressed, his beliefs would take him out of the game and he would quit. I began to ask him a series of questions to find the source of his BS.

"So, what is your biggest concern?" I asked.

"My health," he said. "I know I need to lose weight, but I have no energy, and to be honest, I am working out but I am tired all the time. I am not losing weight, and it's hard."

Once I heard him say it was hard, I knew that there was a Belief System taking over, so I kept probing.

I asked, "What's hard? The workouts or is there something else?"

He said, "I own a very successful company, but my employees seem to be in competition with each other. They are not working together. I feel like a slave to my office because if I leave, nothing gets done. I have to do everything myself. I want to get out more, but I fear that if I leave, everything will implode."

Then I asked, "What if the reason that you are exhausted from your life has nothing to do with your work or even your employees? What if I were to say that everything you are experiencing is stemming from a Belief System, and it's that which is draining you of your precious energy? What if all you need is to change your mindset, and by doing that, restore your energy? What if workouts, or even work, didn't have to be hard, and that you may be creating the space for it to be hard by doing more, when you should be doing less to achieve ultimate results? However, we need to unpack your beliefs to scratch that record. Basically, to tell a new story about your life."

He said, "Okay, wonderful... but how? How do I change my BS and live my life differently?"

I said, "Well, I do it through an 8-step process. I call it, "Unpacking your beliefs." And step one is what you have just accomplished. Step One is: What is the problem? For you, Danny, it's that you're doing lots of work and not seeing results. You're burned out, and you have to do everything yourself. So, write that down!"

This brings us to Step 2:
If it's Hysterical, It's Historical.

I asked Danny, "So, when do you remember feeling for the first time that you had to do everything yourself, that everything was hard and that, no matter what you did to accomplish your goals, you did not see results?"

"I don't know," he said.

Usually, that's the first response I hear to that question. That's because the unconscious mind is being exposed, and its first defense is to push the question aside and pretend not to know the answer.

So, I asked him, "Well, if you did know, what do you think the answer could be?"

He said, without missing a beat, "My dad was a drug addict and alcoholic, and I had to step up and take care of him when I was a kid. I was the grown-up and he was the child. I didn't want to step up. It was too hard, and it didn't really work. He never got better and he died. To this day, I feel responsible for his death. If only I could have tried harder to save him."

I said, "Now we are getting somewhere. Write that down!"

This leads us to Step 3: What was your Belief System at the time?

I asked Danny, "What was your Belief System around having to step up with your dad?"

Again, Danny said he didn't know. So, I helped him here. Many people truly don't know what their BS is, so I asked him a question I learned from a self-help book I read.

I said, "Try saying, 'I'm not.... And the world is....'"

He said, "I don't get it."

"No worries," I said. "I will illustrate with a story. I remember when I was almost three years old. My parents left me at a Shakey's Pizza. At first, I thought it was really cool. However, I soon realized they weren't coming back. By the grace of God, somehow, I managed to tell the police officers how to get me home. It took a long time, but we found it. When I arrived home, over seven hours later, the officer asked my parents if they were forgetting anything. They said no. Then I popped my head out and said, 'Hello.' Once my parents realized they had left me, they then proceeded to shame me for getting lost. 'You should have paid attention,' they told me. In my young mind, I made it mean that I was not lovable, and that the world is very punishing. I made up that story in my head and made it come true with every future relationship, friendship, and even at work. So again, Danny, what did you make it mean based on your specific incident?"

He said, "I made it mean that I am not enough and that the world doesn't support me. As a result, I determined I had do everything myself, because it wasn't safe to rely on my father. I also felt like I wasn't capable because, no matter what I did, my dad continued to drink and use drugs. As a result, I made it mean that I was not enough because if I were, my dad wouldn't have to get high all of the time."

I said, "So basically, no matter what you did with regard to helping your father, it didn't work. That seems to be the same exact pattern or story for your weight and your business, yes?"

"Yes," he agreed.

"Great insight!" I said. "Now write that down."

Now we are making progress, and that leads us to Step 4: What are the consequences of this belief?

Danny was really catching on.

He said, "Well, my health. I have a digestive disorder that causes me to have chronic pain, especially when I eat foods that trigger it. I also have diabetes due to my diet. Next, my energy. I feel burned out all of the time. Then, my relationships, my work, my self-esteem... EVERYTHING... This BS affects EVERYTHING!"

"Okay, great, Danny. Write that down!"

We now arrive at Step 5: What is the payoff of having this BS?

Danny said, "What do you mean? There is no payoff for feeling miserable."

"Oh, but there is," I said, "there's a big payoff! If you were to dig deep, what do you think a payoff for having this belief could be?"

He insisted, "There is absolutely no payoff for having this BS."

Most people are confused when I ask them this question. They will usually tell me at this point that there couldn't possibly be any payoff for having their BS.

I told Danny, "Hang in there, you've got this. The payoff means, 'what is your BS protecting you from?'"

Danny thought for a moment. "Well, the payoff could be that the drama of my life is a deterrent, keeping me from moving forward. When I'm stuck, I don't have to put myself out there, and if I don't step up in my business, then I won't have to assume more responsibilities. In addition, in my workouts, if I lose the weight, then I would be letting go of my favorite foods that comfort me. And, my weight is my protective barrier from myself and the world. Which we have already determined does not support me. I guess my thought is, who would I be if I didn't have this weight on me?"

"Very good insight," I said. "Now write that down."

I said to Danny, "At this point, many self-help gurus would say, 'Aha! You have a fear of failure.' But I don't think that at all. In fact, I know you will succeed and progress, and I think you know you will, too. Does that thought terrify you?"

Danny gave me a puzzled look. "What do you mean?" he said.

"You had to step up as a kid, which was too much responsibility for you. The same applies to your business today. It seems you are stuck, not because you are afraid to fail, but because you don't want the responsibility of taking your life or business to the next level. It represents your father, and it will yank you right back to that childhood situation. It already has, wouldn't you say?"

Danny sat for a moment processing this information. "Yes! That's it." It seemed he exhaled years' worth of worry in that one single breath. "I don't want to take everything to the next level because I feel it will take me out of the game of life. I am already in chronic pain from the stress of my job, and I feel it will cost me my life if I continue."

I interjected, "Just like it cost you your childhood."

"Wow," he said, "I had no idea!"

I said, "What if I told you that if you did less you would be able to become more? Everything would be so much simpler for you, but you would have to manage your energy to do it."

He said, "Okay, I'm in. What do I have to do?"

I said, "We need to come up with a new empowering belief. One that serves you instead of disempowers you. I'll use this as an analogy. Imagine there is a man who is an alcoholic father. His two sons are grown, and one has also become an alcoholic. This son claims he has become an alcoholic who is horrible to his kids because of his childhood with an alcoholic father. But you ask the other son, and he says, 'I am an amazing dad who takes the time to learn good skills so that my kids never have to go through what I went through because I had an alcoholic father.' Both men had an alcoholic father, but they have two different perspectives. One says life happened to him; the other has learned to make life happen for him."

I continued, "As the story says, Danny, my belief is that you wouldn't have gotten to this level of success if you hadn't developed the survival skills you needed to keep you going. However, those same survival skills that got you this far are now killing you. We need to change your mindset so you can sustain your success. Basically, we need to get you out of survival mode and into thriving mode."

"How do I do that?" he asked.

"Basically," I said, "If you're going to make up a story about your life, let's make it a good one. Because your life didn't just happen to you... It happened for you."

> "The moment you take responsibility for everything in
> your life is the moment you can change anything in your
> life."
>
> —Hal Elrod

That brings us to Step 6:
What is your New Belief?

I asked Danny, "So, instead of that child making up a story that he was not enough, that he was unlovable and that he had to do everything himself, what is a new belief that you can have about that child?"

Again, Danny told me he didn't know.

Again, I said, "If you did know, what would the answer be?"

"Well," he said, "I guess the new belief would be that I am resourceful and I know how to get the job done!"

"Great!" I said, "What else?"

He said, "I guess I could have another belief that I am enough."

"Wonderful" I said, "Give me one more."

Then he said, "Another belief is that I can and will attract others around me to do their part, so I can let my guard down   and relax a little bit."

"That's it!" I said. "Now, let's come up with a new belief about that world. What could the world be for you?"

"I could believe that the world is very supportive and available to me," he said.

"Beautiful! Let's write that down."

That brings us to Step 7:
What is your solution?

Danny agreed that he was now ready to step up in all areas of his life, so I asked, "Is there anyone that you trust who can help you right now?"

"Yes," he said, "I have a wonderful team of people around me. I just have a hard time knowing what they need to do and what I need to do."

"Okay, so you need to become clear on your employees' job descriptions and your description. What else?"

"Well, I need to add self-care into my lifestyle. I also need to set up boundaries and say no to certain people and delegate my work," he said.

"Wonderful!" I said.

And so, at last we reach Step 8: Visualize using all five senses!

It was time to help Danny complete the final step on the path to installing his new belief system. I asked, "Now that you have new beliefs and a solution, what does your new life look like?"

"It looks like me wanting to go into work, feeling amazing, and my employees not needing me as much," he said. "It looks like me being in the office less, free."

"Wonderful, and if that feeling of freedom had a texture, what would it feel like?" I asked.

"It feels like tree bark, tough exterior for protection, and yet smooth on the inside." he said.

"And if that vision of freedom had a smell, what would it smell like?"

"It would smell like fresh pine trees in the mountains. Fresh, crisp, and clean."

"And if that vision of freedom had a sound what would it sound like?"

"Like a gentle breeze blowing through the trees."

"And if that vision of freedom had a taste what would it taste like?"

"It would taste like a soothing cup of homemade chicken soup."

I asked, "How does taking your life to the next level feel now?"

"It feels comforting, free and exciting!"

That was music to my ears!

After that session, Danny hired me to come into his office and help him clarify his executive team's job description. He also hired me to facilitate group meetings to ensure everyone was communicating effectively and operating on the same team. Within three months, Danny had created a strategy for his self-care plan, as well as developed a method for financial freedom. He also tripled his income, and he's not stopping there. The sky's the limit, baby! He built a rocket ship, and is blasting off to the moon!

* * * * *

Now that I've shown you how I helped Danny, I want to guide you through the same process for your life. I know this is a lot of information, and if you feel you still do not understand this chapter, don't worry. The next several chapters will be dedicated to digging deeper into each step. Stay with me!

Let's delve deep into unpacking your excess baggage. You can only bring eight items, and "identifying" them is the first step. It all begins when you notice a situation that is triggering you. In Danny's case, he was feeling overwhelmed and burned out about his company. He also felt as if he was stuck, unable to move forward, and his efforts brought little or no results. However, it wasn't his work environment that was draining him. It was the projection of a situation from his past into the present. So now let's begin with you.

Step 1: Identifying Problems— What is a problem you are dealing with now?

Do you become triggered when a certain person says a certain thing? Do you continue to attract a certain situation over and over again? For example, do you attract the same kind of intimate relationship, or attract friends who are a takers? This was true in my own life. I kept attracting the same man in a relationship in a repeat cycle. Even though they were different men, they all had similar possessive, emotionally draining, controlling personalities. This cycle wasn't only occurring in intimate relationships; I also attracted friends who were the same way—always wanting to borrow money, or trying to make me feel bad or wrong if I didn't give them what they wanted. They were energy vampires who leached off of me. Why? They all represented my mother. It's what I grew up with and what I was used to.

So, what is it for you? Are you burned out, stressed out, and overwhelmed with your life? Do people treat you a certain way that you would like to change? Do you have chronic worry or stress about what others think? Whatever your situation is, identify it and write it down.

Step 2: If It's Hysterical, It's Historical.

When do you remember feeling this emotion in the past? What was the very first time you felt this way? In Danny's case, his employees were not stepping up, but that particular issue wasn't the first time he had experienced someone or something not supporting him. That experience began in childhood with his father, who wasn't emotionally or physically available. Danny carried the BS created by this experience everywhere he went. It was that computer program running in the background, and even though he couldn't see it, that programming continued to drain the battery of his life-force. It ran day in and day out, through his business life, his personal life, and even affecting his health, sucking his energy dry. However, it wasn't the actual business doing it; it was Danny's underlying belief about the company that replayed like the movie Groundhog Day over and over again. At least the film only repeated itself for two hours. His internal movie lasted his entire life; that is, until he was able to wake up to his new perception.

Once Danny became aware of what he was projecting, the rest was easy to shift. Some say that awareness is 90% of changing a pattern because you cannot change what you do not see. Once he became aware that there was a BS in play, and that he was creating it, he was able to open his eyes to the story he had been telling himself and change it to a story that suited him. Basically, if he was going to make up a story of his life, he might as well make up a good one. Once he unpacked the daily rituals that created such negative results, he was able to see which thought process was causing it. Then, he was able to plant new seeds to create a mindset shift and ultimately achieve his success.

So, let's delve into what Step 2 is for you. Remember, if it's hysterical, it's historical. What, from the past, does your present situation remind you of? If you think you don't know, ask yourself, what if you did? Write it down.

> *"We cannot solve a problem with the same mind that created it."*
> —Albert Einstein

Step 3: What Meaning Did that Belief System Have for Me?

People often cling to habituated beliefs about themselves even when new events occur that might cause them to reconsider or re-evaluate their beliefs. They tend to remain embedded in the groove of their old self-referencing thoughts and patterns. These beliefs and images are typically born out of early experiences from childhood and continue to define the way we see ourselves, blocking out opportunities for positive change. Every single one of us has had something painful happen to us in childhood—a friend rejected us, a parent scolded us, we might have failed a test—and those events caused a Belief System to form. We then created a story around that belief and made that experience mean something negative about us or the world, or both. Typical examples are stories that go something like this: "I am not good enough;" "I am dirty;" or "life is hard, and I have to do everything myself." The trick would be to understand those events and create stories that reflect reality. However, when we are children, we don't know any better because, at that age, everything is about us.

For example, when Danny was a child, his dad was an alcoholic and wasn't available to step up at times. What Danny made that mean about himself was that he was not enough, that nobody had his back, and that he couldn't trust anyone to do their part. So, he had to do everything himself. Once this BS was created, Danny carried it with him everywhere he went and literally developed a life to fit that story. He basically handed everyone a script of how he wanted them to act, and when that person played their part, his story was reinforced, keeping him stuck in his BS. Basically, your BS causes you to attract what you don't want in your life: that which you resist persists.

Brad.

Another example of this comes from Brad, a client I had. We were doing a goal-setting workshop and I asked him, "What do you want? What is your goal?"

He said, "I want to become big and strong."

"How come?" I asked.

He said, "Because the chicks dig it."

I said, "Why do you want chicks to dig you?"

He said, "Because I don't want to be dominated or manipulated."

I said, "Is that what you are attracting now?"

He said, "How did you know?"

I explained, "When someone doesn't want something, it's usually what they attract, and if you do not come up with a new belief system, you will continue to attract what you don't want over and over again. And, even though you don't want this to happen, we can't come up with a new belief if we don't even know that we have the old belief. So, when was the first time you can remember having this belief, and what did you make it mean?"

He said, "Well, my mother was controlling and told me what to do all the time. She never gave me the space to be myself. I always had to perform for her love. No matter what I did, she still made me wrong."

"Got it!" I said. "And what was the belief about yourself that you created?"

"I made the story mean that I am weak, not enough, and I will never get it right no matter what I do."

"Very good insight," I said. "Write that down."

The same thing that happened to Brad had happened to me. The story I used to tell myself was that I had been placed on this planet to be used and abused. I believed I was meant to be a victim, unlovable and unworthy. Was this true? Absolutely not. However, I continued to feel unworthy and created an environment where I attracted the same kind of experience within relationships—with business partners, with my husband, and even with my child. In each relationship, I became a doormat. I worked really hard to please everyone, walking on eggshells, bending myself into a pretzel, and trying make everyone happy. What I got in return was abuse, aggression, and punishment. What I didn't realize was *I* was the one creating the script, and *I* was the one putting myself in these situations over and over again, thinking each time it would be different. Some people say the past doesn't equal the future. I say, "Of course, it does if you keep doing the same thing." Only when we can identify our BS, then we have the power to change the future for the better.

Now it's time to complete your own Step 3. In Step 2, you remembered what happened in the past, and you wrote down that experience. For Step 3, think about what that experience meant for you: what story did you tell yourself about who you were? Write it down.

Step 4: What is the consequence of that belief?

Of course, what you believe has consequences. It could impact finances, personal relationships, your self-esteem, your health, or something else. In Danny's case, his belief affected his finances because he couldn't take his business to the next level by himself. It affected his health with a stress-induced digestive disorder and diabetes, it affected his personal relationships, because he attracted unavailable partners who would eventually leave him, and it even affected his weight because he kept a protective layer of fat around his body. It affected every part of his being. In what areas of your life does your Belief System affect you? Write them down.

Step 5: What is the payoff of my belief?

It could be as simple as "I feel good about being right!" You'd be surprised what we will do to keep living in that old life/lie so we don't have to move on. There is a definite payoff in thinking negatively. It's like an emotional hit of heroin. For example, in Danny's case, his BS kept him stuck, and the drama of his life was a blinder, so he didn't have to move forward. If Danny had moved forward, in his mind it meant he would have to assume more responsibility, which he determined felt daunting and unstainable, and that would yank him emotionally right back to childhood.

Some people don't want to change simply because there is an emotional payoff from playing the victim. It may be a way to receive attention. Another payoff is that of familiarity and comfort. However, when you come down from the high that payoff provides, you have to create more drama or another big emotion so you can get that hit again. Our goal is to identify the payoff of the old belief or pattern. Then we can move you out of this unhealthy cycle and moving on and into your beautiful new life.

There's one last thing about Step 5. Many of my clients tend to be hard on themselves when they identify their hidden beliefs. But don't make yourself feel in the wrong regarding the past, not even one little bit. You didn't know any better. When you know better, you'll do better. So, to reiterate, never make yourself wrong. Do your best to quickly identify the old BS, so you can move out of it and into the solution. That brings us to Step 6. Let's create a new belief!

Step 6: What is my new Belief?

To create your new belief, let's look for the opposite of the old one. For example, if your belief is, "I am not enough and the world is punishing me," write down the opposite of that. You could write, "I am enough and the world is a safe place." At first you will think, "BS! Literally, bullshit! That's not true." However, you can encourage your mind to agree with you by asking yourself "why" questions to help with the process. What are the "why" questions? Success coach Noah St. John calls them "Afformations." Yes, that's correct, afformations, not affirmations. What's the difference?

An affirmation is a statement that you say over and over again to try to trick your brain into believing it's true. However, I feel that affirmations only work if you already believe what you are saying, which kind of defeats the purpose. Usually, the people who say affirmations don't believe what they are saying. The brain then says, "this is bullshit" and rejects the affirmations. A typical affirmation might be "I am enough." However, an afformation is a "why" questions about the statement. By asking yourself, "Why am I enough?" you move past all the filters of the mind, past the need to prove anything to yourself, and access the unconscious directly. Why? Because the brain LOVES to solve problems. Sometimes it even creates them just so it can solve them. When someone asks a why question, the brain will get to work in finding the solution to why you are lovable, why you are enough, why you are amazing, and why the world is safe. If you don't believe me, try it for a week and watch the miracles that take place in your life. I will cover this further in a following chapter, but for now, what are your New Beliefs? What are your new "Why" questions? Write them down.

Step 7: What is my solution?

Now we are getting you out of your old story and into a solution. Remember that the brain LOVES to solve problems. When you ask your brain what your solution is, at first, it will say, "I don't know." Give it a minute, and soon the answers will start flooding in. The solution for Danny was to first come up with a new belief, and then ask himself why questions. Then, he added his busy schedule into his self-care plan, not the other way around. This helped him clear his mind and freed up his energy so he could think straight. Lastly, he needed to become clear on his job description and the job descriptions of his employees, and he needed to establish his boundaries and stick to them. So, what is the solution to your challenge? Write it down.

Once your solution is clear, we want to move into mental imagery. This means asking yourself, "What would my life look like if I were living in the solution?" For example, I used to work with professional athletes. Sometimes I would video their games. Once the game was over, we would immediately watch the footage. We would see the mistakes they had made. Once the mistake was identified, I would immediately ask them, "What could you have done to prevent that?" They would write down the answer. When finished writing, I would have each athlete visualize their solution and how they would have liked to perform. This visualization exercise worked wonders. I often use this in my own life and with every client I work with. I even do this with my daughter when she is having trouble with a friend or with schoolwork.

Step 8: Write down your solutions and what you want your life to look like.

Write down your solutions and what you want your life to look like, and write in present time, as if it has already happened. When you talk in present time, you begin to plant the seeds of your new reality into your unconscious mind. You have lived your old lie for so long that, if you don't plant new seeds, you will immediately revert back to your old life. When you visualize, you tell your brain, "This is what I want. Get to work on this now." I call this mental imagery a dress rehearsal to help you move through bumps smoothly. For example, you might be someone who has social anxiety and feels fear in meeting new people and talking to them at a party. Visualize what you want to have happen. Once you address the anxiety in your meditation, it's easier to face your fear and integrate healing into your life.

We have now taken you through this simple 8-step process that has moved you past the barrier of big emotions and through to the other side to your powerful new self!

Step 1: What happened? Write it down.

Step 2: If it's hysterical, it's historical. When do you remember the first time feeling this way? Write it down.

Step 3: What is your BS? Write it down.

Step 4: What is the consequence of your BS? Write down.

Step 5: What is your payoff? Write it down.

Step 6: What is your new BS? Write it down.

Step 7: What is your Solution? Write it down.

Step 8: Visualize your new life! Write it down and read it every day!

In the next chapter we are going to go over what adrenal fatigue is and discuss some simple solutions to help you gain your energy back!

CHAPTER IV
Recovering From Burnout and Adrenal Fatigue

Why is it so much harder to make it through the day than it used to be? Where did my energy go? Most importantly, how do I get it back? If you are asking yourself these questions, please know that you are not alone. Millions of people just like you are trying to figure out why they feel drained throughout the day. The answer? You may be suffering from adrenal fatigue. Adrenals are the little glands that sit on top of the kidneys. These glands are very important for brain health, weight management, glowing skin, sufficient energy, and adequate sleep. If not taken care of, these glands can contribute to many avoidable diseases, as well as to depression and a lack of energy.

I could devote an entire book to adrenal fatigue alone; however, I will condense this chapter into eight simple steps to "reverse the curse." Before we start, I want you to answer some questions. If you answer yes to three or more of these questions, it's more than that you are suffering from adrenal fatigue.

- Are you a caregiver?
- Are you always on the go and possibly looking like you've aged more than you should?
- Do you feel overwhelmed most of the day, even when there isn't really anything wrong?
- Do you have dark circles around your eyes?
- Do you have a tendency to gain weight, especially around the middle, the waist?

- Are you tired throughout the day? In other words, do you feel exhausted in the morning upon waking, even if you've slept eight hours?
- Do you have brain fog or feel sluggish and scatter-brained, especially between the hours of 2 to 4 p.m.?
- Do you feel lightheaded when rising from a lying down position?
- Is your sex drive noticeably lower?
- Do you crave foods that will momentarily make you feel good, even though you know they will make you feel worse later, after you crash?
- Do you feel depressed or unexcited about your past hobbies?
- Do you feel wired even though you're really tired?
- Do you wake up between 1 and 4 a.m.?

You have just discovered the symptoms of adrenal fatigue. To explain what is actually happening when your body is triggered, picture this: A deer is chillin' out on a Sunday afternoon, eating some grass in the woods with its deer family. All of a sudden, it hears a noise in the bushes. The deer pops his head up and sees a pack of wolves is nearby. Bam! Immediately, the deer's autonomic nervous system kicks into hyper alert. The immune system shuts down, digestion shuts off, the cognitive function to the brain shuts off, the muscles in his central body shut off, and the central nervous system to the brain begins to pump adrenaline throughout the body. It forces blood to the extremities (the legs) to prepare the body to run in case it needs to flee or fight. Or the deer might freeze and become motionless trying to blend into the surrounding forest environment to hide. During that intense hyper-state, the only things the deer can think about are 1: Where is the predator? 2: Where is my escape route? 3: How much time do I have to get to safety? And that's it. Absolutely nothing else! However, once that deer is safe, everything goes back to normal within about an hour and a half. Most animals can endure that short-term stress for a little while, and in some cases, stress is actually a good thing; it keeps us on our toes. However, when we experience stress on a regular basis, it creates imbalance and begins to break down the body.

One of my favorite authors is Dr. Joe Dispenza. In his work, *Breaking The Habit Of Being Yourself*, he says it perfectly:

> When you react to something in your life, you turn on a primitive nervous system called your fight or flight nervous system. The moment you perceive a threat in your external environment, your neo cortex sends a signal to the limbic brain which sends an electro-chemical signal down the spinal cord to turn on the adrenal glands.
>
> Once the adrenal glands are turned on, they begin to secrete a certain amount of adrenaline. The moment adrenaline is released into the body, there is a physiological change. The pupils dilate, the salivary juices shut down, your heart rate increases, the respiratory rate increases and the blood is sent to your extremities to prepare you to fight, freeze, or run.
>
> But the danger doesn't have to be a saber tooth tiger. It could be your mother-in-law. Now you are viewing your mother-in-law as a predator and, based on the past, you're seeing her as the threat.

Now, let's picture a typical day for a working mom who's trying to get her kids off to school. Kids don't want to dress themselves, let alone get out of bed. By the time everyone rushes out the door, mom is frustrated and overwhelmed, and everyone is late. While driving the kids to school, mom is on the phone, trying to send an email while the kids are eating breakfast in the car, and it's off to the races we go, go, go. Then she has to deal with the carpool lane. Heaven forbid someone cuts her off. By the time she gets to work, she's lucky if she's eaten anything. More than likely, she grabs a cup of caffeinated coffee, or two or three, because she is already exhausted from her morning. As a matter of fact, she woke up exhausted even though she had eight hours of sleep. She arrives to work by 9 a.m., blankly starring at the mound of tasks that need to be done right away. Her work load should be given to a team of people. However, most of the burden has been placed on her.

Hallelujah, another work day finished! However, now, it's time to pick up the kids, make dinner, and help kids with homework. Then, Hip, Hip, Hooray, it's time for the kids to go to sleep! Mom might have time for a TV show and a glass of wine, or two or three, to help her unwind. She finally crawls into her beautiful, amazing bed. Thank God, the day is over! She begins to snuggle close to her pillow. Oh, her beautiful, amazing pillow. As she drifts off to dreamland, she can finally let her guard down and fully relax. Oh, thank God for dream time. Then she feels a hand caressing her shoulder. Oh, hell no! It's her husband or partner initiating intimacy. She looks at him and cringes. He wonders why she rejects him and can't understand why she becomes bitter and resentful when he tries to touch her. This mom is burned out! On a side note, when men ask me how to turn on their wives or partners, what I usually say is, "Take out the trash and help her around the house." The best aphrodisiac is helping with chores and carrying some of her work load.

Going back to the adrenals, remember their purpose is to help you keep alert and keep you alive. When the body turns on this energy, it is ready to deal with whatever condition is challenging it. This is a good thing and contributes to growth if the stress happens every once in a while. However, humans tend to create an over-stimulated nervous system. The adrenal hormone produced in response to a problem sends a chemical rush that makes the body feel alive. Because of this, stress can be highly addictive. Just by thinking about problems, the body can create a sense of euphoria and will continue to create crises just to get this hit of adrenaline. Over time, the body can become addicted to the emotional rush. The more addicted you are to your emotions, the more likely you are to continue to think the way you think, thereby reaffirming your problems and continuing to receive that emotional hit.

When you're thinking about a particular problem—say, the fear of what might happen in the future—your body begins to memorize that anxiety. Then, your body can become anxious without you. An example of this might be when you're hanging out with your kids, playing at the park, and all of a sudden, out of nowhere, comes the thought, "How am I going to pay for their college education? I have three kids and college is so expensive." Bam...an anxiety attack pops up out of the blue. Not dealing with stress, letting your body get out of balance, and spending too much time in emergency mode can lead to serious health problems. Eventually, you will run out of energy, and the cortisol produced by your adrenal glands will punch holes through your immune system.

When there is no energy in your internal environment, you are more vulnerable to mental disorders like anxiety, depression, and obsessive disorder. In addition, you may suffer from digestive disorders like IBS, acid reflux, and Crohn's Disease as well as autoimmune disorders, colds, heart disease, diabetes and even cancer. Chronic stress can also contribute to an unpleasant condition called "leaky gut." Leaky gut, also known as increased intestinal permeability, is a digestive condition in which bacteria and toxins are able to "leak" through the intestinal wall. Little tears develop in the intestinal lining, allowing food and bacteria to seep through. The body's immune response considers it foreign matter and sends antibodies to attack it. As a result, one may experience food sensitivities that cause pain and inflammation throughout the body, even if they eat only organic healthy foods, because the body sees that leaked food as a threat.

Now you understand that the negative emotional stress we create—and may even be addicted to—can cause serious health issues. How did we get into this painful mindset to begin with? We live fast-paced lives and sometimes just barely manage to keep up. In addition, I have noticed a common trait among my "Type AA" personalities who are over-achievers. Most of them suffer from anger, judgment, fear, anxiety, unworthiness, pain, and depression. At an unconscious level, they are plain mad. Why you might ask? Most of my over-achievers in life had to step up during childhood when they didn't want to. Either a parent, friend, coach, or someone left them holding the bag, and they had to take the lead. As children, they perceived that if they didn't, they wouldn't survive. They were trained to stay in what I call a survival mode and developed unhealthy survival skills, which worked for quite a long time. Eventually, though, those survival skills that worked at one time become the very thing that holds them back, and that is softly, or not so softly, killing them.

Let's get straight into the important work of calming the body down on a daily basis. I learned this for myself and use it when working with most of my clients, especially those with cognitive disorders. Many gurus would say: "Just meditate." I say: "Are you frickin' kidding me?" The last thing I would have someone in a panicked state try to do is meditate, especially my clients who have schizophrenia. What do you think would happen if I had someone, who is hallucinating or having a panic attack, sit down and meditate? They would lose their shit. I can guarantee you it wouldn't be pretty. In my experience, when someone is in a panicked state, I need to have them move that kinetic, wiry energy out of their body.

"If you are in a bad mood go for a walk. If you are still in a bad mood go for another walk."

—Hippocrates

For example, if a client is in a hyper-intense state, I have them walk or move their bodies, preferably outside. Once we moved that kinetic energy up and out of their body, I have them lie down, breathe deeply, and put their feet up on the wall at a 90-degree angle. Why would I do this? Remember, when the body is in a hyper-intense state, the adrenals push blood into the extremities. When one lies down and puts their feet up onto the wall for 15 minutes, the body draws the blood out of the extremities and back into the heart. Once the blood is forced back into the heart, the body will begin to calm down.

Next, I have my client lie on their side, place their head on a pillow, and open up their top arm. Why? Think about it. If the ceiling came crashing down on me, what would I do? I would close off my chest, and protect myself with my back. When one is in survival mode, the chest closes in, the shoulders roll forward, and the back begins to hunch over. (On a side note, have you ever noticed how our bodies are beginning to hunch over earlier in life these days? Our bodies are molding into our chairs, and we are turning back into our cave-dwelling ancestors.) Okay, back to getting you out of a state of hyper-intensity. When we lie on our side with our top arm open, a message is sent to the central nervous system saying, "I would not be lying here, completely open, if I were being chased by a saber tooth tiger." The body will then begin to relax, and the immune system, cognitive brain, muscles, digestion, and everything else will reconnect and turn back on.

If my client is still feeling anxiety, I have them complete the 8-step writing assignment from Unpacking Your Beliefs, (because, remember, if it's hysterical, it's historical). Then, I would have them take a hot bath to further calm the body. It works, it really does. Remember, I suffered from PTSD from the severe trauma of my childhood. These are all things that helped me, and I know they will help you, too.

Some of you might be saying, "But it can't be that simple." I say, "It is that simple." However, it may not be easy because getting yourself to do these things may be like pulling teeth. Why? Why don't we remember to add self-care when we are going through stressful experiences? I remember a client saying to me, "I have the resources to have a massage, or to 'roll out' and do other self-care things, but I just don't. Why not?" Of course, he couldn't. He was paralyzed by that fight, flight or freeze mode.

Let's go back to our friend the deer. If that deer is being chased by a pack of wolves, is it going to want to stop and get a massage? Of course, not! All he is thinking is 1: Where is the predator? 2: Where can I run for safety? 3: How much time do I have to get there? He is in survival mode. Humans are no different and still continue to have that reptilian brain response. All your body knows is to flippin' run! No questions asked. It doesn't know the difference between, "I'm stressed-out taking the kids to Disneyland," and, "That saber-tooth tiger is gonna eat me!" It just knows... Adrenaline! And many humans are living in that survival mode from the time they wake up in the morning till it's time to go to bed at night.

Maslow's Hierarchy of Needs

I like to use Maslow's Hierarchy of Needs to demonstrate how some life essentials must be established first. Psychologist Abraham Maslow created a pyramid graphic to illustrate his theory of what people need, first to survive and then to thrive. In Maslow's Hierarchy of Needs chart, there are five levels from the bottom up:

> Level 1: Physical Needs—does the person have food, water, and shelter?

Level 2: Safety—is the person safe? Is a predator after them?

Level 3: Love and Belonging—is the person able to give and receive love and be part of a community?

Level 4: Esteem—does the person have self-esteem, usually achieved by doing things they feel are estimable acts?

Level 5: Self-Actualization, the last and highest level on the pyramid—is the person calm enough to allow them to improve their connection to a High Power?

Wellbeing depends on meeting the needs in sequence so that survival basics are satisfied first. One cannot even begin to allow love in, even self-love and nurturing, until those first two needs of physical requirements and safety are met. As a result, most people feel numb to life, because when you numb out pain, you also numb out happiness. The body doesn't know how to just numb out fear, worry, and stress, so people walk around numb, pushing down their pain and fear with addictions or neurosis. They can't calm their central nervous system down enough to allow love in. For example, if that deer is being chased by that wolf, is he going to be able to relax and enjoy having a nice meal and a meaningful conversation with his deer family? Again, no! Do you think the deer would even be able to digest that meal when he is in this hyper-intense-state? All he can think of is, "How am I going to survive?" And that's how most of my clients feel. They say, "I know my family loves me, but I feel alone and unable to let their love in." Why?

My theory is that if you have to numb emotional pain, you also have to numb joy. You can't numb one without numbing the other. Most of my clients' motherboards to their brains are so fried that they have no feeling, other than wiry anxiety or depression/suppression. Because they are in that fight-or-flight state all the time, their brain and body will begin to predict the future based on the past, and that is how their thoughts can make them sick. Exhausting, isn't it? It happens in moments. And, even though the adrenaline rush they receive comes and goes in moments, the stress hormone cortisol it brings with it can last for days. In time, it begins to break down the immune system.

Now you know what adrenal fatigue is. I have already given you a few things you could do physically, so here are a few things you can do to help calm your adrenals down on a daily basis to begin the repair process for your new life. Again, I am giving a few simple steps in this chapter. The rest of this book will give you your larger blueprint for living.

> *"If you want a new outcome, you will have to break the habit of being yourself and reinvent a new self."*
>
> —Joe Dispenza

Solution:

1. After dinner, go for a walk. High intensity workouts are not good for you in the evening. Slow movement is better. Walk, breathe, and practice walking meditation. Walking bare foot in nature can be grounding, too.
2. Lie down and put your feet up on the wall. This allows blood flow to come back into the heart.
3. 8-Step Writing from Unpacking Your Beliefs. Use the 8-Step Writing exercises from Chapter 3.
4. Proper Sleep. Set a bedtime ritual and do the same thing every night. Dim the room. Take an Epsom salt bath with essential oils. Lavender is very calming.
5. Turn off electronics 1-2 hours before bed.
6. Read, Write, Meditate. (You'll learn more about this in a later chapter.)

7. Take vitamin supplements that support adrenal health, including Magnesium, B Vitamins, Vitamin C, and Glutathione.
8. Nutrition (which we will talk about in a later chapter).

In our discussion of adrenal fatigue, we've learned that your thoughts can make you sick. Why? Because we begin to fry the motherboard of our brain. Let's begin to retrain that brain and start living the life that we love. In the next chapter, we will talk about energy drains and how to get rid of them.

CHAPTER V
Tired of Being Tired? Identifying and Clearing Your Energy Drains

*"It isn't the mountain ahead to climb that wears you out;
it's the pebble in your shoe."*
—Muhammad Ali

Do you feel like you have enough energy throughout the day? Or do you feel like you're barely making it? Even if you sleep eight hours, do you wake up feeling refreshed, or are you dragging yourself out of bed to face another day? You may know you have the potential for great energy, but you may not know how to activate it. In this chapter, we will talk about what drains your precious energy and discuss tips and solutions for removing those drains. Let's get started!

Energy Drain #1: Closets

When you enter your home, car, office, or closet, how do you feel? Does it feel inviting and warm, or do you experience anxiety or an uneasy chaotic sensation? Maybe your home looks clean and beautiful, but you have closets, drawers, or a garage filled to the gills with things you never ever use. We love our things. However, when we keep unnecessary clutter around us, it fills our brain with unnecessary clutter to match. It's like a laptop computer. You may only be able to see one or two programs open on the screen, but there are several others draining your battery. The same goes for the clutter in your home. Basically, the bulge is taking over the background space in your brain. If you can't think straight, chances are it's because you have too much going on in the clutter department. Let me illustrate with a story.

Jane.

Jane came to me and said, "You know, Kim, every time I walk into my bedroom closet, I feel like I have anxiety. I don't know why. Would you please come with me and help me clean out my closet?"

Now, I'm not a professional closet cleaner, but I love this woman and wanted to help her feel better. So, I went to her house and walked into her closet. I could feel it, too.

I asked her, "Can you tell me a little bit about what's going on in your closet? For example, first tell me about your clothes." I pulled out a ragged old shirt that was ripped in the front from neck to bottom. I asked, "What is this? It looks old, and it's ripped. And what's this stain on the front?"

She looked down with a very sad expression. Clearly, I had hit a nerve. "That's the gown my mother was wearing when she had a heart attack and passed away. And those stains are blood."

As I ripped my hand away from the garment—and pulled my jaw off the floor—I responded in what I felt was the best matter-of-fact voice I could muster, "Ooohh, okay, got it!"

She continued, "And these are all my brother's things from when he passed away, and, oh, these are the papers with my sister's obituary as well. And these are the outfits that she used to wear."

My heart felt for this woman. She had lost her mom, her brother, and her sister within two years of each other.

"No wonder you have anxiety, angel," I told her. "All you can see in your closet is death. We have to get this stuff out of here. And this blood-stained garment needs to be thrown away now."

And that's exactly what we did. We went through Jane's clothes, shoes, belts, papers—anything that was in the closet. We made a "love it," "leave it," and a "maybe" pile. And the "maybe" pile went to the "leave it" pile.

I said, "If you don't feel fabulous in it, toss it because otherwise you'll feel the negativity, and that will drain your energy." What a healing she experienced after we were finished! She donated eight huge heavy bags to the Goodwill, which would contribute to someone else's well-being. Then she painted her closet and burned some sage to further clear the energy. After we were finished, when we walked into her closet, it felt amazing. It was her very own sanctuary, which created space in her brain for other hopeful, healing things.

Every season, I do the same thing in my home; I clean out every drawer, even junk drawers, and my closets and even my pantries. I even tell my daughter, "You know, if you don't feel good in it, let's get it out of your closet because it's just going to sit there and take up precious space, not only in your closet, but also in your head." I need my home to feel amazing because, guess what? This is my safe sanctuary. If it does not feel good when I come home, I'm not going to be any good to you or anyone else. My home represents my brain, and when it's not clear then I'm not either. I know it can seem overwhelming to clean out your closets, especially when they are bulging with clutter. Here are a few tips to get you started:

Solution:

1. Start with a junk drawer—small, simple, and easy to do.
2. Set a timer and clean that closet for 15 minutes. If you want to stop after that, you can. Set aside 15 minutes a day until you're done. You'll be surprised at what you can get accomplished in just 15 minutes.
3. Have a friend come and help you.
4. If you're too embarrassed to have your friends see your bulge, hire someone to help you.

Energy Drain #2: Environment

Your environment includes all that surrounds you—your home, your work, even the restaurants and bars you visit. The environment you surround yourself with is very important. I'll focus on your work environment here since we've just talked about the closets in your home. You want to make sure that, if you're working eight, ten, or twelve hours a day and you're under fluorescent lights, you take regular breaks by getting outside and refreshing your energy. Studies show that nature is one of the key components to our well-being, especially when people work under florescent lights. In addition, vitamin D deficiencies can occur from lack of exposure to the sun.

For your after-hours environments, consider how night clubs and bars are filled with second-hand smoke. Also, many low-energy people hang out in bars. That doesn't mean you shouldn't go out and have a good time. Just make sure you add the self-care element so that when you do, you can recover easily from it.

Solution:

1. Add some plants to your office environment. Dress up your space with pictures that make you happy.
2. Get up from your desk and go for a 10-minute walk outside in nature.
3. Eat your lunch outside. Get outside as often as you can!
4. If you can't get outside, open a window.
5. When you walk into an environment, ask yourself: Does this feel good to me? If it feels good, then it is a good environment. How you feel lets you know the kind of environment you are entering. When you go out to have a good time, be mindful of where you go and who you will associate with. Which brings us to Energy Drain #3.

"You cannot expect to live a positive life if you hang with negative people."

—Joel Osteen

Energy Drain #3: People/Energy Vampires

Many clients ask me, "Does it really matter who I have in my inner circle? Does it really affect my business and my life?" I say, "Absolutely." When you begin the process of letting your old life go and implement this new way of living, something will happen. You will develop this light about you, and just as many bugs are attracted to the light. It's up to you to choose who to have in your space. Many people will either try to possess your light, suck it from you, steal it from you, or try to dim it. They think that light is coming from you, but it's not. It's coming from the connection you have to your Higher Self. It's called your vitality, your life-force, and when you begin to connect with your Higher Self, you will shine brightly. Many people do not understand that it cannot be taken from you, nor can they possess it, even though they will try. They can only obtain it by doing the work necessary to connect with it for themselves.

Once you have that life force, it is your job to protect it. As you begin to grow, you might notice that you become more sensitive. Relationships you once were able to tolerate may not be tolerable to you anymore. Your friends may not like the new you as you become more aware and more connected to your inner Self. When you become connected to your inner child, you may become more sensitive. That's a good thing. However, you want to make sure that you protect that sensitive child and be the kind of parent you wish you'd had or would like to be. In this way, you will now determine who that child can play with, and you will keep that child away from predators and energy suckers. That child is the key to your stable future, and if that inner child doesn't feel safe, he or she will revert to making your life a living hell.

That being said, have you ever had the experience of feeling fine *before* you spend time with a certain friend, family member, or co-worker? Then, when you left the meeting or session, you felt exhausted, as if the life had been sucked right out of you? I call these people "Energy Vampires." Energy vampires are very real and they are everywhere. When you have been in contact with an energy vampire, you may feel lethargic, irritated, overwhelmed, anxious, and exhausted, but you may not know why you are feeling this way. How can you determine if you are hanging around energy vampires? You'll know it because your energy is depleted after being with them. What can you do?

Solution:

Here are some things you can do to eliminate or minimize your negative experiences with these energy vampires:

1. Get clear on your boundaries and stick to them. You must get clear because energy vampires can always find a way to make you wrong for setting limits and boundaries. They will even throw tantrums, use guilt trips, or bully you to get what they want. When you know what your needs are and stick with them, energy vampires will eventually stop trying to get their way with you because they will see that it doesn't work anymore. They might express a big emotion because you're not co-signing their BS. But guess what? You'll have more energy as a result.
2. If an energy vampire is gossiping about someone or complaining, a solution could be to say, "Oh, I'm so sorry to hear that." Then change the subject to a lighter topic—a TV show or even the weather. If they continue to bring the conversation back to their woes and worries, politely

let them know that you have to go and get the heck out of there.

3. Lastly, if you can't get away from an energy vampire, make sure to add self-care into your lifestyle so that you can let go of the negativity when you leave them.

Energy Drain # 4: Lack of a Schedule

I have written an entire chapter on planning later in this book, so I will be brief here. I used to ask myself, "How am I going to fit my workouts and my self-care plan into my busy life?" Now I ask myself, "How can I fit my busy life into my self-care plan?" What that does is allow me to make sure that I'm getting self-care scheduled into my life on a daily basis. If I do not add self-care into my life, then I burn out. Having a schedule is super important because you won't have to spend your precious energy thinking about what you are going to do next. When your schedule is written out, it saves the necessary energy, so you can sustain being available to the daily tasks at hand, including being productive at work and taking care of the people around you.

Solution:

1. Buy a little daily planner that you like and write out your self-care plan. Then schedule your day around that. When you make small deposits of self-care throughout the day, you will have enough energy to help you enjoy the day without becoming exhausted.
2. Look at your plan each morning and each evening to keep on track.
3. Be light-hearted about your plan. Sometimes, it can feel like a leash is tied around our necks, but when you can have fun with your planned schedule, it won't feel so daunting.

Energy Drain #5: Nutrition

What would happen if I put sugar in my gas tank? It would blow up my engine, yes? If it didn't blow it up, it would definitely ruin it. Your body is no different. What you put into your body determines the maximum output you achieve. Now, I have also dedicated an entire chapter to nutrition, so I will keep it simple here. Eat foods that are nutrient-dense and fuel your body.

A great formula for a meal would be:
- 3 oz Organic Protein—chicken, steak, fish, tofu, etc.
- 1/2 cup cooked brown rice—1 cup if you are a man. If you are not consuming grains, 1/2 yam or potato—1 whole yam or potato if you're a man, or 1 whole piece of fruit.
- 1 Tbsp of healthy fats and oils—olive oil, coconut oil, avocado, almond butter, peanut butter, ghee butter, etc.

For a snack
- A small handful of almonds, or
- 2 Tbsp hummus with some veggies, or
- 2 oz of turkey with 1/2 of an avocado

The formula for the day would be
- Breakfast
- Lunch
- Snack
- Dinner
- Snack

You can read more in my nutrition chapter on examples of food choices and times to eat.

Energy Drain #6: Exercise

By exercise, I mean either lack of exercise or too much. When we exercise, we want to create a balance. Think about it. If you are always on the go, go, go and working, working, working, do you think it's best to create a kick-your-ass workout program? Ah, no! Your body is already burned out. The last thing I would do is put you on a workout regimen that knocks your immune system down even further. If your adrenals are burned out, or if you haven't worked out in a while, you want to ease into your program. Later in the book, there is an entire chapter dedicated to exercise. There is a Three Cycle System that I have used for my clients, and now I have made it available to you. Additionally, if you want a well-rounded program with videos, you can go to my website, KimberlyLou.com, and click on the Repair—Rebuild—Recover program.

For now, just know that we need to start implementing exercise slowly at first—the kind of exercises that will allow the adrenals to relax. Start out by performing mild steady-state cardio, such as long duration walks, mild hikes, or riding a recumbent bike, three times per week for no more than 30 minutes for the first two weeks of your program. Sometimes people get bored with this cardio, but it's what the adrenals need. Slow and nurturing. Also, a restorative yoga class is great. Not a full-on yoga class; the body is not ready for that and may become injured. I see this all the time. Although yoga is a wonderful way to calm down your central nervous system, every single one of my clients, including me, has become injured due to the moves in yoga. I would say to wait until your body has recovered, and then begin your yoga routine. Until then, I would exercise with weights or do Pilates instead.

In my experience, weights and Pilates are best at first because with every pound of muscle you gain, you will lose 50 additional calories per day. Now don't worry, women, we're not talking about big muscle gain. Again, I have some videos on how to work out—especially if you're just getting started.

Solution:

1. For two weeks, perform steady-state cardio three times per week—walking, recumbent biking, mild hiking in nature (the body loves it any time you do anything outside and in nature).
2. Once you are ready you can: Lift moderate weights Mondays, Wednesdays, and Fridays. Mild cardio on Tuesdays and Thursdays. No more than 30 minutes to 1 hour max.
   - Monday - Moderate weightlifting: back and biceps
   - Tuesday - Mild cardio
   - Wednesday - Moderate weightlifting - legs
   - Thursday - Mild cardio
   - Friday - Moderate weightlifting: chest and triceps

Once your body becomes stronger, you can pick up the pace and add a more rigorous program.

Energy Drain #7: Sleep

Many people burn the candle at both ends. When they are crunching to get a project done, sleep is the first thing to go. Also, insomnia is an ongoing epidemic. Many suffer from not being able to sleep due to stress-related problems. In addition, cognitive problems begin to raise their ugly heads when the brain is sleep-deprived. Your brain won't function properly and may become foggy. Dr. Itzhak Fried, a professor of neurosurgery at the University of California, Los Angeles (UCLA), said, "Starving the body of sleep also robs neurons of the ability to function properly. This paves the way for cognitive lapses in how we perceive and react to the world around us." He went on to say that, in his studies, as the patients became tired, it became more challenging for them to categorize images, and their brain cells began to slow down. Unlike the usual rapid reaction, the neurons responded slowly, fired weakly, and their transmissions dragged on longer than usual, causing mental lapses. For example, when a sleep-deprived driver sees a pedestrian stepping in front of his car, it may take longer for the driver to realize what he or she is seeing because "the very act of seeing the pedestrian slows down in the driver's overtired brain."

In addition, lack of sleep will not allow the body to recover as quickly. A Harvard study stated that the body must sleep seven to nine hours of every day. Additionally, the best times to sleep are from 10 p.m. to 6 a.m. The hours from 10 p.m. to 2 a.m. are for brain recovery, and 2 a.m. to 6 a.m. is for body recovery. A solution to creating a better night's sleep is to create a bed time routine. It's what I do for my daughter to ensure she gets to bed on time. First, we have dinner, then bath time. Story time is next, then soft music. We do this every single evening and, before you know it, she's asleep. Even when we're grown up, we still need that routine.

Solution:

1. Turn off all electronics one to two hours prior to bedtime
2. Take a hot shower or bath
3. Read, write, meditate
4. Play soft music with a timer so it turns off within 30 minutes
5. Sleep from 10 p.m. to 6 a.m. if possible

Energy Drain #8: Negative Thinking

Your thinking is very powerful, and just as you must build your muscles at the gym on a consistent basis, you need to take the same care of your mind. Thinking is the biggest component of your energy recovery program and your life. So many people are sloppy with their thinking, or they may believe there is no use in trying to try to change it, because it won't work. I am here to say that you can retrain that mental muscle, just like any other muscle. We often have Belief Systems that keep running, like a laptop computer program without our awareness. The brain is your motherboard, and your Belief Systems are the programs that take over, whether good or not so good. We must become clear on the Blind Spots that hold us back. That means we must turn those other programs off. Once you do that, you can maintain that motherboard and begin to exercise your mind on a daily basis.

That first hour in the morning is especially important. Your first hour is gold, so use it wisely. How do we do that when we're programmed to think of something negative when we wake up? Here are a few things to help redirect your mind toward the life that you love.

Solution:

- Gratitude. Yes, I said it… Gratitude! It really does work. When you begin your day with "Thank You," the Universe listens. Focus goes where attention flows. Write down ten things that you are thankful for and watch how that redirects your attention toward a more positive mindset.

- Meditate 15 minutes in the morning and, if you can, 15 minutes at night. By doing that, you are planting positive seeds for your new life and for your future to grow.

- Ask yourself positive "why" questions, then sit back and listen for the answers. The brain loves to solve problems, so when you ask yourself "why" questions, you slip through those old filters into the solution processing center of the brain. "Why do I feel so good?" Your brain will come up with answers and solutions for you every time.

- Be of service. I remember watching a Tony Robbins interview. He spoke about how we usually derive happiness only for a short time from the things that we buy—up to six months max. Then we lose interest. However, we create real fulfillment through the experiences that we have. I know this is true from my own life. When I am feeling afraid of the future or in a "lack" mentality, I focus on being of service. This means opening the doors for people. Giving someone a compliment. Paying for someone's coffee behind me in line. When we bring joy to other's lives, it gets us out of our own head. When we get out of our own head, even for just a moment, we can come back to our challenges with a fresh mind. More than likely, when we have a fresh mind, we can see our situation with a re-energized brain and clear eyes.

Come to my YouTube channel, Kimberly Lou, or to my website, Kimberlylou.com. I have created a community so you don't have to do this alone. I created this community for a reason. I wish I'd had something out there to tell me what I was experiencing and what to do. I couldn't find it, so I created it for people like me, people who wanted to do the work but just needed to be pointed in the right direction.

There you have it—eight energy drains.

Energy Drain #1: Clutter

Walking into a cluttered space can drain your energy. Take fifteen minutes and just start. Reorganize and clean your closets, junk drawers, computers, desk, even your car, especially the middle console.

Energy Drain #2: Change up your Environment

If you are working 8, 10, 12 hours a day sitting under fluorescent lights, add plants, fun pictures, colorful objects you love, to brighten your day. Get up and go for walks, preferably in nature, to lighten your mood.

Energy Drain #3: People/ Energy Vampires

One of the most important things you need to know is that certain people can and will drain your energy. You want to be very mindful of who you are surrounded by. Set boundaries, change the subject when they become negative, and limit time with low-energy people. Remember, birds of a feather flock together. Be mindful of who you hang around with, because who you hang around with is who you will become.

Energy Drain #4: Keep a Routine

Plan your day and plan your play. Ask yourself, "How can I add my busy life into my self-care plan? When you have a regular self-care plan, your body can sustain your bigger life purpose.

Energy Drain #5: Nutrition

Your nutrition is super important. The type of fuel you put into your gas tank is going to determine whether you can sustain your lifestyle. Make sure to eat nutrient dense foods to take your rocket ship to the moon.

Energy Drain #6: Exercise

Too much exercise, or not enough, can drain your energy. Create a well-balanced plan that is sustainable. If you need help, go to KimberlyLou.com to find the most appropriate plan for you.

Energy Drain #7: Sleep

Sleep at least seven to nine hours, preferably between 10 p.m. and 6 a.m. to sustain your fast-paced lifestyle.

Energy Drain #8: Your Thinking

One of the most important determiners of your energy is your thinking. Your thinking alone can drain you of your precious energy. Try to build a new mindset on a daily basis, just like you would build muscle in the gym. Remember that first hour of power in the morning. Use it wisely meditating, writing, and practicing mental imagery by visualizing your future. Plant seeds for a positive day.

CHAPTER VI
Tap Into Resources You Never Knew You Had

Let's talk about reading, writing, and meditating. You may ask, "What do reading, writing, and meditating have to do with building a better body?" I say, EVERYTHING! As *New York Times* best-selling author and neuroscientist, Joe Dispenza, says, "Meditating is a means for you to move beyond your analytical mind so you can access your unconscious mind. That's crucial, since the unconscious is where all your bad habits and behaviors you want to change live."

We've already talked about unpacking your Belief System and creating a new one. Now it's time to lay a solid foundation for your new life by accessing your unconscious mind and planting positive seeds for the habits and behaviors you want to grow. The best times to plant those seeds into your unconscious mind is during the first five minutes upon awakening and the last five minutes before you retire at night. A paragraph from Rick Warren's *A Purpose Driven Life* illustrates this idea:

> *"It all starts as a seed, whether it's your time, money, appreciation, wisdom, or energy. Your words can also be seeds you plant in people's minds. They grow and they bear fruit. So, you need to choose your words wisely, especially when you're talking with people you love, like your children, your husband, your wife, and your friends."*

He explains why these seeds matter:

> *"What kind of seeds are you planting in your relationships? Are you planting seeds of trust, or are you planting seeds of distrust? Are you planting seeds of kindness, or are you planting seeds of crankiness? Are you planting seeds that build up, or are you planting seeds that tear down? Remember: You will reap whatever you sow."*

Here is how I practice this principle with my morning meditation steps:

Step 1—Read: I find something to read that motivates or inspires me, that plants a seed into the unconscious mind and says, "This is the positive direction I want my mind to go." When we plant the seeds of what we want, our unconscious mind goes to work, and after a while, we see the evidence of those seeds growing.

Step 2—Write or Journal: Next, I either write about what I just read, so that my thought can be set in stone, or I journal about my feelings or my day ahead to help clear out negative thoughts. Many of us harbor negative thoughts and emotions of jealousy, resentment, frustration, and even stress. Most of us hold that in. What that does, however, is drain us of our precious energy. When we journal about what's inside us, it helps us release whatever it is and move that big emotion out of our body. Then we can restore our energy and clear out our minds. This allows us to prepare fertile soil to plant new, more positive seeds.

Step 3—Meditation: There are many wonderful types of meditation, including transcendental and mindful, and even yoga practices like Kundalini. Over time, as you become more advanced in your program, you can consider enhancing your meditation practice. Now, though, the meditation I am talking about is just plain sitting still and listening to the surrounding environment. That's it. Many of my clients say, "Kim, I don't know how to meditate, and I'm not a person who can just sit around." Believe me, five minutes of silent reflection goes a long way, and you don't really have to do anything. Just stop and listen to the surrounding environment. Let's practice now. Close your eyes, take a deep breath and hold it. What do you hear? For me, I can hear my refrigerator humming. I can hear the air conditioning blowing. I can even hear my heart beating. Now exhale. There you have it, folks. That is meditation. Being in the moment and noticing the surrounding sounds is all it takes to begin achieving a clear mind and a calm energy.

Step 4—Breathing: Before we move on to other meditation practices, let's talk about breathing. Tanya J. Peterson, MS, published an article for HealthyPlace.com which discusses the relationship between breath and mental health. In it, she stated:

Intentional deep breathing improves mental health by relaxing both the body and the mind. Taking slow, deep breaths increases oxygen in our bloodstream and thus in our brain. Deep breathing signals the parasympathetic nervous system to activate and thus induce relaxation throughout the body. When we breathe deeply, our heart rate slows and our blood pressure decreases.

Often, my clients ask, "How do I breathe?" And, "What position should I sit in while meditating?" Some people like to breathe in for the count of four through their nose, hold it for the count of sixteen, and exhale through their mouth for the count of eight. Other people just like to breathe normally by inhaling through their nose and exhaling through their mouth. Use whatever pattern feels more comfortable for you. The point is, just breathe. As far as your sitting position, sit in a chair and place both feet firmly on the floor, or if you'd rather sit on the floor in a cross-legged position, that's fine, too. The idea is to be comfortable. Next, rest your hands on your knees. You can place your thumb and index finger together, but that's unnecessary if you would rather not.

Now that you know what meditation is, let's take five minutes and practice. Sit comfortably, close your eyes and take a deep breath through your nose and hold it. Then, let it go. Again, inhale through your nose and hold it. Then, let it go. Take the breath in, hold it and let it go. Then, repeat your breathing five more times.

Next, focus on your heart. Feel the rhythm of your heartbeat. What does it sound like? What does it feel like? Just notice. Now, listen to your environment. What do you hear? Maybe the air-conditioning? Maybe the fridge? Whatever it is, just listen without judgment. Then, inhale and hold the breath. Let it go. Again, another deep breath in and hold it. Let it go. Then, just breathe normally and notice what else you hear.

If you notice racing thoughts pushing their way in, don't resist them. Whatever we resist will persist, which means those things will become stronger and louder and take over your entire meditation if you let them. Just acknowledge them by saying in your mind, "I see you. I hear you. You can leave now." Then center yourself back into your breath. Continue by taking a deep breath in, holding it and letting it go. Now, your meditation is on track.

Next, focus on your heart again. You can even place your hand on your heart, if that helps. Feel it beating. It's super simple. What does your heart need? Take a deep breath in and hold it. Let it go. Another question you can ask yourself is: what do I need right now? Take a deep breath and hold it. Let it go. Then, just sit quietly and listen for the answer. Whatever comes to you is perfect. Focus back on your heart and listen. What do you hear? Now, bring your focus back to your body and realize your surroundings. Slowly, wiggle your fingers and your toes, and then when you're ready, you can open your eyes. How do you feel? Beautiful.

So, that is meditation on a basic level. And honestly, it need not be more complicated than that, especially when you're first starting out. The main thing is to find a little time each day to quiet your mind and your heart so you can really listen to what you need. This self-care plan is sustainable. As you add self-care, you will create a lifestyle and a body built to thrive for a LIFETIME.

That being said, we have so much going on throughout the day. Remember that the first five minutes in the morning and the last five minutes in the evening are the most important times when your mind is receptive; the soil is fertile and ready to absorb the new positive seeds you will now plant and ultimately grow. Tony Robbins said: "Most people do not understand the giant capacity we can immediately command when we focus all of our resources on mastering a single area of our lives." So, let's create that ritual to achieve your most amazing life by doing the following:

Step 1: Read something inspirational or motivational

Step 2: Write/Journal your thoughts

Step 3: Be still and listen to the surrounding environment, which will help you gain greater clarity on the action you need to take.

Practice these 3 steps as we progress through this program and see what amazing new gifts open for you. Sometimes big emotions may pop up for you in this process. What we have to realize is that feelings are not facts. They come up and threaten to take us out. But really, they are simply emotions. If we sit with an emotion for a moment, it will disappear. Relax, feel the emotion, and it will disappear out of your body.

The next chapter deals with Collapsing Emotions. We will discuss how to do this. I can't wait for you to see the new life that is waiting to emerge through you!

CHAPTER VII
Emotions are Energy

"Anything that you fight with or struggle against grows larger. You give power to lower energies by focusing upon them. You don't eliminate darkness by arguing with it. The only way to eliminate darkness is to turn on a light."

—Doreen Virtue

By now, you should be realizing that Emotional Fitness is the key to managing your life-force energy. I cannot put you on an exercise and nutrition routine before these steps are complete because, in my experience, if Emotional Fitness is not there, you will not be able to sustain your new lifestyle. For staying power, we first need to retrain your brain and determine what drains your energy. Many thoughts and emotions threaten to suck the life-force right out of us, and then we wonder why we cannot manage our lives. So, before we get into the exercise portion of this workbook, I want to talk about one more very important thing: Big Ass Emotions!

I have worked with over 10,000 people at either a one-on-one or group level. Many have struggled, filling their lives with addictions including food, alcohol, drugs, workaholism, and sex, all of which impacts their health. In many cases, these addictions led to self-destructive behaviors, creating painful lives in addition to destroying some of the closest relationships around them. Another way my clients have destroyed them-selves is by caring for the people around them to the detriment of their health and well-being; this can also be an addiction. I see this time and time again. There is an epidemic of people running away from anything that causes them to face the truth of their own lives—they are running from their inner demons, if you will. I call these inner demons Big Ass Emotions.

What keeps people stuck in this vicious cycle, causing them and their loved ones to suffer? It is a survival mode which stems from childhood, especially for those who had to step up as children and take responsibility. There was a past pain, a hurt, that they now spend their lives trying to avoid. As a result, they stay stuck in a Belief System, a story which they assigned a meaning to. They unconsciously hold onto the negative energy of their past, and they can't let it go because they don't even know it's there. These survival skills have worked for many people for a very long time. However, this survival mode, that has helped them in the past, comes at a great cost.

The pain of the life-lie keeps the central nervous system on high alert and causes people to stay stuck in a vicious reptilian-brain cycle that never allows the mind to rest. Because of this, many people (at least 15% of the population) are suffering from severe depression. Even more suffer from mental disorders like PTSD and anxiety. Their central nervous systems remain in a fight or flight mode, pushing them to the extremes in order to avoid feeling their "Big Ass Emotions." Many find themselves developing neurotic coping mechanisms like acute or chronic anxiety, depression, obsessive–compulsive disorder, fixations, and addictions. These coping mechanisms cause a plethora of stress-induced ailments in the body like adrenal fatigue, autoimmune disorders, irritable bowel disorders, diabetes, heart disease, and cancer. This shocking conclusion saddens me. I have lost friends and family to curable disorders that—if they had allowed themselves to release the past and added self-care into their lives—would have been able to heal, create new lives, and sustain themselves for the long haul.

Why did this loss happen? In many cases, there was an underlying feeling of shame. They felt they were bad, not enough, or wrong. That's why they pursued such extremes, trying to run away from the pain of their past and struggling to fill that unfillable gaping hole in their hearts. There is, however, a simple solution. It's called feeling those *Big Ass Emotions*. When people will themselves to turn around and face their feelings, especially the ones that they have been running from their whole lives, what they will usually find is that *Emotions Are Just Energy*, and those emotions will usually fade away within five to ten minutes. I call this *Collapsing an Emotion*. I'm not sure where the phrase was first coined, but I like it, so I will use it.

Let me illustrate with a story.

Jackie.

I remember when I was a child, I would often have this recurring nightmare. In my nightmare, a witch would chase me down the street and around the corner while I was on my way to school. This witch was fast, and the more I tried to run, the heavier my legs became. It was as if I were running in quicksand. My dream ended the same way every time—the witch would catch me, and I would wake up in a panic, drenched in a pool of sweat.

This dream haunted me for many years. However, I vividly remember the last time I ever had this dream. I was running as usual, and I heard this voice that ordered me to turn around and face that witch. As I turned around, I puffed up my chest, looked her straight in the eyes and said, "No more! You're done now!" She had a surprised look on her face. She was used to me running away from her. Then she melted away and was gone forever. I had faced my inner demon, my Big Ass Emotion. Once I did, she disappeared never to be seen again.

Fast forward to my adulthood. I was sharing with my client, Jackie, how I thought emotions were not real, that they were just a bunch of kinetic energy that had built up without an outlet.

She asked me, "What do you mean by that? My emotions certainly feel real to me."

I said, "Just because they feel real doesn't mean they are. They are just energy. I'll illustrate with "The Dog Whisperer" Cesar Milan's philosophy. He asks this: if you keep a dog closed up in a house all day with no exercise, no structure, and no purpose, what will happen?"

She said, "The dog would probably eat my shoes, tear up my couch, or worse."

I said, "Exactly. Also, in Cesar Milan's book, Be the Pack Leader, he speaks about how dogs develop anxieties, fixations (addictions), and many other disorders, and if we do not create an outlet for that dog to channel that energy, he will become destructive. Humans are no different, especially when they have a Belief System tied into that pent-up energy."

I continued, "The intense emotions people feel are usually caused because there hasn't been an outlet for them to express these emotions in a way that is healthy. What happens as a result is that they suffer. But the suffering is not real. It's only the result of the meaning they've placed on their experience. For example, what does this treadmill mean to you?"

She said, "Pain!"

After I stopped laughing, I said, "Yes, that is the meaning that you've placed on the treadmill. However, other clients of mine might have said that it is their sanctuary, or that it's boring. Are any of those statements real? Absolutely not! This treadmill is just a hunk of parts that don't mean anything until we assign it meaning. And that's what painful emotions are—kinetic energy without an outlet resulting from lack of structure and from assigning meaning to the story we tell ourselves. Viktor Frankl stated it so beautifully: "Suffering only comes from the meaning that we place on the story." This treadmill is just a box with parts. It's not painful until you place the painful energy onto it."

"For the meaning of life differs from man to man, from day to day and from hour to hour. What matters, therefore, is not the meaning of life in general but rather the specific meaning of a person's life at a given moment."
—Viktor Frankl

"However, in life there is pain," I said. "For example, if I cut my finger, will I experience pain?"

"Yes, of course!" she said.

"Exactly! Then where does the suffering come from?"

She said, "Oh, I see it now. The suffering comes from me dwelling on me cutting my finger."

"Exactly!" I said, "We don't suffer until we give the emotion way too much focus and energy. I'll give you another example in my own life. I remember going through a divorce. I was terrified to take a break from my ex-husband. My emotions were so intense that my body began to have a physical reaction. I was in my car driving. In hindsight, I should have pulled over, but I kept driving while I witnessed my body experiencing anxiety and fear. I felt dizzy and like I was going to pass out. I soon realized my body was moving through a big experience of withdrawal. It was so intense it felt like I was going to die. However, I knew in my head what was happening. Even though my body was clearly having a physical reaction, I knew it would pass, and that I would be fine if I didn't resist it. Because, remember, whatever we resist, persists. So, I just sat there and let my body move through all of my Big Ass Emotions. Rage, anger, fear, resentment, and worry. Even though they were intense, after about fifteen minutes, my body started to calm down. What I felt next was incredible—a sense of complete peace. In the moment, if felt like a lifetime. After that, I knew that collapsing emotions really worked. However, it only works if you are ready to fully experience and feel the emotions. That's why many people stay stuck in their lives. They are afraid that intense feeling is going to kill them. That's why they resist. And we can check out and resist life in so many ways. Procrastination is a way to check out and *resist. Burning the candle at both ends, being like a hamster on a wheel going nowhere fast, is a way to resist and check out, too."*

Jackie asked, "Is that why I constantly push myself to do more, even when I don't want to?"

"It could be!" I said, "When we are workaholics, that is a way to check out. Overeating, alcoholism, isolating, talking too much, spacing out, and binge-watching Netflix are all ways we check out. We also check out to keep ourselves distracted from our Beliefs Systems, to keep from discovering the truth about ourselves because, at an unconscious level, we associate pain with taking our lives to the next level."

Why do we check out when we really want to take our lives to the next level? Because, to some people, it seems like way too much responsibility to be present and feel their emotions. It seems really scary to change, so they avoid it. That being said, we have developed neurotic behaviors to keep us from experiencing ten minutes of pain, which keeps us from the truth. What we don't realize is that the truth will set us free, and the responsibility of facing our fears is the very thing that will liberate us.

However, to get to that freedom, we must face our inner demons by sitting down and feeling our Big Ass Emotions; these usually only take five minutes to collapse, fifteen tops. When we collapse those emotions, in most cases, our pain will disappear. Many people say they want to change and take their lives to the next level. However, most do not want the responsibility it takes to be successful. In my humble opinion, deep down, every overachiever secretly doesn't want the responsibility they have. It's too much, and many people stay stuck because they feel safe in the known. They think it would be a lot to face if they had to roll up their sleeves and do the emotional work needed to take their lives to the next level. That is why they will get to a certain level in life, or work, even in their workout routine, and then quit. Our Belief System (inner child) is absolutely driving all of that behavior.

It's kind of like "battered wife syndrome." I have worked with many abuse survivors who kept going back to their spouses before they worked with me, because the old life, even though very traumatic, was familiar. However, when they can get in touch with the truth about what is happening, they can do something about it. The truth will literally set them free. The truth is that their survival skills worked for and protected them in the past. But those same survival skills don't work anymore. Not even one little bit. As a matter of fact, they are the very thing that is holding them back, or maybe even killing them. They have to get honest about how they have been acting. Only they can bring the trouble to light and heal it. When we can realize the common denominator to all of our problems is us—that we created these problems by the very energy that we hold—and when we stop living in denial and get honest, growth happens. Every time!

That is their personal freedom. Their joy. They can't feel joy if they continue to lie to themselves; it's like putting a happy face sticker on an empty gas gauge, as my favorite author Esther Hicks would say. Usually, unless there is a chemical imbalance (and often even then), when they turn around and face their Big Ass Emotions, at first it will feel like they are going to die. However, just like in my dream, the emotions are not real and have no power unless they are given power.

> *"To manage our emotions is not to drug them or suppress them, but to understand them so that we can intelligently direct our emotions energies and intentions…. It's time for human beings to grow up emotionally, to mature into emotionally managed and responsible citizens. No Magic pill will do it."*
> —Doc Childre

So, my job is to teach you the tools to be able to identify that kinetic energy, redirect it, and channel it into your new purpose and the life you love. My question to you is, "*Do you want success?"* Because it is simple, but not easy. This is why, unconsciously, many people would rather fail than succeed. Even though they could succeed, and the rewards would be immense, they may perceive it as a harder way to live with more responsibility and the continued work of self-improvement. That work, however, is the very thing that will set them free and bring them joy.

Most people think the idea of fearing success is ridiculous. How could anyone living the life of wonderful vacations, creature comforts, and easy habits find it hard? But that's not what my multi-billionaire CEOs are afraid of. To them, the thought of being a whole person means never giving up on themselves, even when they feel like they are not worthy. It also means being big enough and whole enough to be there for others when they feel the same way. And what is scarier than other people depending on you and looking up to you while you are thinking, "If they found out who I really am, they would run"?

It's true that people who are successful have to face their fears on a regular basis. Fears come and go, but once you realize that fears are not real, and are only False Evidence Appearing Real, then it becomes easier to turn those fearful thoughts into a more positive outlook. And that is the point of this book. It is to prepare you for your success and to help you lay a solid foundation, so you can realize your FEAR is just kinetic energy needing to be channeled properly through a creative healthy outlet. Fears are not real!

> *"Just as physical energy comes from diet, exercise, and rest, emotional energy comes from the ways you take care of yourself emotionally—living in a way that makes you feel inspired, hopeful, self-confident, playful, loving and in touch with what you care about most."*
> —Mira Kirshenbaum

Exercise:

Now that you know that your Big Ass Emotions are not real, let's face them, redirect them, and channel them into a life you love. This means collapsing an emotion. In most cases, it will take no more than fifteen minutes for the Big Ass Emotions to fade away. Many people spend their entire lives trying to avoid these fifteen minutes of pain and cave in to a craving. I am going to help you confront your fears, expose them, and let them go.

So, find a space and sit quietly. Turn off any phones that go ding and make sure no one will interrupt you. We are going to begin with how I taught you to meditate by noticing the sounds around you. It could be the air conditioner, the fridge, maybe there are cars passing outside your window. Next, I want you to scan your body. Start from the top of your head to the tippy tips of your fingers and toes. Notice what part of your body is talking to you. Is it your stomach? Do you have energy in your chest? Maybe the energy you are feeling is in your head. Wherever it is, feel it. Don't let it get away from you. Sometimes, the energy will change and the sensation will move to a different part of your body. This is completely normal. What the body is trying to do is trick you to get you to stop feeling the energy around it. Just stick with it and follow wherever the energy in your body goes. Home in on it and feel it until it completely disappears. Sometimes, the body will try to throw you off track, and you might start to feel physical symptoms like a sense of anxiety. Stick with the energy you feel and it will disappear.

There have been times when my clients continue to feel the Big Ass Emotion, and say, "I can't do this anymore, it's too much." It's okay if you can't do it in just one sitting. What I recommend is that you collapse your emotions in increments and over time; it will still be effective. The objective is to make sure to feel the emotion fully and, in most cases, until it is completely gone, leaving you with a sense of peace. Some clients ask me, "How will I know it is collapsed?" That's easy: you will feel that energy disappear and you will feel a sense of peace.

It really does work. If you are having trouble with this technique, you don't have to do this by yourself. I have a guided meditation called "Body Sense" that you can find on my website, KimberlyLou.com, which can help you.

Now, that we have learned to collapse an emotion, let's look at the workings of The Universal Language of Energy—the subtext behind the words we speak.

CHAPTER VIII
The Universal Language of Energy: The Subtext Behind the Words We Speak

"Energy doesn't communicate in English, French, Chinese or Swahili, but it does speak clearly."
—Elaine Seiler

Now, I love me some Cesar Millan! I have been watching him for years. I resonate with his message because he talks about how life is all about energy and how the world that we create around us is dictated and affected by the energy that we carry within ourselves. I have known and felt this energy since I was a child. However, I was never able to put a name or words to what I was feeling, and eventually teaching, until I read his book, *Be the Pack Leader*. The name of this energy? The Universal Language of Energy.

With this Universal Language of Energy, Cesar speaks about how when animals—in his case dogs—develop neurotic behaviors and addictions, it's a result of instincts gone awry: basically, pent-up energy without an outlet. Whether we are dogs, humans, or snakes, when we hold that energy inside, we transfer it into everything that comes into our space, especially negative energy. However, if we can learn to harness that chaotic kinetic energy, transmute it, and redirect it towards our projects, we can use it to skyrocket our dreams into a harmonious reality and live the life we love.

In the past, I would try to describe this energy to people around me. Often, they wouldn't understand what I was trying to say. At first, they would think I was asking them to be like a Tibetan monk, meditating at the mountaintop. Of course, that was not what I was talking about at all. I would then strive to explain that when I was talking about energy, I was talking about the subtext behind the words that people speak. For example, humans are the only animals in nature who can say one thing and mean another. An example is when someone smiles to your face then turns around and gossips behind your back. Because of this, our actions and our outcomes are the real language we should be listening to, not words.

In the animal kingdom, what you see is what you get. For example, what would happen if you approached a dog with a fearful energy? You'd probably say it would try to bite you, try to dominate you, or ignore you by putting its back to you. If these are your answers, you are absolutely correct. Why would the dog do this? Because it felt your fearful energy. Now let's change the scenario. What would happen if you walked up to that same dog with a calmer, more assertive energy? Something quite different, yes? That same dog would either chill out with you, maybe lick you; he certainly wouldn't bite you. You see, all animals have the ability to communicate. They communicate through a language more like telepathy, or the Universal Language of Energy. They are who they are, and what you see is what you get.

Summer.

I love my daughter, Summer. She is amazing! She's hard-working, funny, and smart, but there is one thing Summer resists. It's called exercise. She was the baby I had to pull out of the stroller and say, "Get out and walk!" If it were up to her, she would be happy to hang out at home all day long and binge-watch Netflix. So, when

I heard about how someone had built fairy houses along a hiking trail, I knew it would be a great way to help her exercise.

And we had so much fun! We skipped, danced, ran, and hiked to each fairy home. Every home had a different fairy in it, and Summer was convinced she would be able coax the fairies out to play with her. It was super cute to watch her tactics. At first, she would sing. When that didn't work, she would cry. Still the fairies would not come out. That didn't discourage her, though, not even one little bit. She would try a different approach with each fairy home she came in contact with.

As we were nearing the end of trail, Summer saw the very last fairy home. She said, "Can I run to it, Mommy?" I said, "Of course," very pleased with myself. As she was running, something happened. It was as if she hit a brick wall. She stood there paralyzed by fear. She didn't say a word, but I knew something was wrong. I could feel it. I placed my finger on my lips motioning for her to remain quiet, slowly grabbed her hand in case I needed to pull her away from danger, and began looking around. I couldn't see anything wrong, but my instincts warned me there was danger close by. Finally, I saw it. A rattlesnake lay coiled up within four feet of us. That snake sent us a clear message which said, "If you come any closer, I will kill you!" It didn't need to use words, and we didn't even need to see this snake for it to get its message across. We received that signal loud and clear through telepathy. Slowly, we both stepped around the snake and got the hell out of there. I'm so grateful my daughter and I are very in tune with our Universal Language of Energy. If not, we could have been dead.

So, how do you think the human race in general is doing with their sense of intuition? The powerful language of energy is always present, but are we tuned in and using it to help us? How do we learn to pay closer attention to the Universal Language of Energy, beginning with the people around us? All of us communicate through energy whether we realize it or not. For example, we could be sending a message that we are weak or desperate, and if we are sending a message that we are weak or desperate, what will we attract? Predators! If we send the message that we are calm and assertive, what will we attract? People who respect us and are calm around us. Have you ever noticed, when you're having a bad day, people treat you with disrespect, and when you are happy, people smile at you more? They are all reading into your energy and responding to it.

So, what's the solution? How do we become better at sending and receiving energy messages? We need to find a way to manage our energy from our internal and external sources. But how do we manage what we don't even know is there? And more importantly, how do we connect to the inner knowledge that gives us the intuition we need to move in the right direction, especially when our lifestyles are super fast-paced and hooked in to our electronic devices, keeping us stuck in survival mode?

We have already talked about our BS and how to unpack it, and we have discussed meditation. We have learned how to get out of survival mode by unpacking our BS and adding quiet time. Especially in that first hour of the day, we can begin to develop a relationship with our inner child who is the source of our chaos. Yes, your inner child is the source of all of your discomfort. When we can meet that inner child's deepest needs and become the parent or mentor we've wished for our whole lives, then they will move out of our way, which will allow us to plant daily seeds and remove those blind spots we don't even know are there.

> *"There is within each of us a child. A child who, to one*
> *degree or another, did not receive the parenting he or she*
> *wanted. There was not enough love or care or support.*
> *We keep looking for someone to be the good parent,*
> *someone to count on... There is only one way to get*
> *superb parenting of the child who will always be within*
> *you. Only one person truly knows what that child wants.*

*Only one person will, or can, love and nurture that child
to the point of peace and joy. Only one person can be the
good mother, father, brother, sister.
You are your best parent and friend."*

—Joan Chittister

Accept, love, and care for the child within you. Beginning in childhood, we create a BS and then carry that energy everywhere we go. For me, my BS started with the experience I described earlier of being left behind by my parents at Shakey's Pizza when I was almost three years old. At first, being at Shakey's alone was kind of cool. I drank as much Coca Cola as I wanted and played limitless arcade games. However, when reality set in, I came to the harsh conclusion that nobody was coming for me. The significance of this experience was the story I told myself about it. What I made it mean was that I was unlovable because, if I were lovable, nobody would have left me at Shakey's. Also, my parents' response made me believe that the world was very punishing. I grew up with this belief and carried it with me everywhere I went, like a sack of rocks. As you can imagine, I took this view of reality everywhere I went and created situations for people, places, and things to prove me right. I used the Universal Language of Energy to say, "Treat me like shit. I deserve it!" What I didn't know I was that I was the powerful creator of this story, not the victim of it. I was the one who continued to draw painful situations into my life with the stories I told to myself and the energy I conveyed behind the words I spoke.

I see this time and again with my clients as well. They create similar stories and self-fulfilling prophecies, and they will not let them go. And, if I try to address the BS too quickly, they will fight me to keep their limitations. That's why it's important to address that four, five, or six-year-old child within as soon as possible because until you unpack your beliefs, that inner child is driving your life. The sooner you develop a relationship with him or her to recognize and include them, the sooner you will be able to get in touch with your instinct and your own Universal Language of Energy. This will, in turn, give you back your intuition.

Some of you may be saying, "You had me at Universal Energy. However, this inner child thing is bullshit." I know, and I hear you. I said the same thing. You might also be saying, "Kim, I just wanted to lose weight. What does the inner child have to do with weight loss or the *Becoming Who You're Meant to Be* Program?" Everything, I say! If you do not take charge of your life-force energy and manage it through Mental Focus, Emotional Fitness, and Physical Training, you will completely deplete that energy and lose your vitality. And, chances are, if you are reading this book, that is what you are experiencing right now. Am I right?

Remember, we are constantly sending messages to the people around us via energy. If we are rejected, there is a reason for it. If we are successful, there is a reason for it. You may have a blind spot that you're not aware of; you must look at what you are attracting into your life in order to know if it's there. When we can recognize the blind spots we have, we can deal with them. It works, it truly does. So, let's learn how to speak a new language—the Universal Language of Energy.

> *"Caring for your inner child has a powerful and surprisingly quick result: Do it and the child heals."*
> –Martha Beck

Exercise:

Because most people can't see their chaotic kinetic energy, I want to break this down into a three-part series.

Part 1: We all have gifts and do well in certain areas of our lives. So, let's start by noticing where you are already successful. Do you find that you are great in business? Maybe it's friendships? Are you a great wife or husband?

David.

I was teaching a class. I asked my students, "Who is good at something?" One of my students, David, said, "I am really good at playing chess."

"Sweet!" I said, "How did you become good at chess? Did you just pick up a chess piece one day and you knew what to do, or did you take classes, or practice?"

He said, "I spent two years with a chess coach, and I practice for hours at it."

I said, "So you practiced a lot and you hired a coach. You didn't just develop this skill overnight, you had to work at it?"

"Yes," he said.

"Wonderful. Is there anyone else who is good at something in this group?"

A few more students stated they were great at art or being creative.

"Wonderful," I said. "Did that happen overnight or did you take classes and practice?"

Without a beat each student said, "We had classes and practiced."

"Again, wonderful! So, would you say there is a formula for success?"

"Yes, there is," they all exclaimed.

I said, "Okay, let's discuss the formula of what you did to become successful and write it down."

Now I say the same to you. What are you good at? Write it down. Once you have written that down, find the pattern. Why are you amazing at what you do? Remember that energy goes where attention flows. What do you do on a regular basis to drive success in that particular area? Write it down.

Part 2: Now, pick an area of life that's not so great for you. For example, how's your weight loss program? How are your finances? What about the relationships around you? Do you get along with the people closest to you or is there chaos?

Stuart.

I asked that same class, "What are you not so good at?"

Stuart exclaimed, "I am horrible at relationships and talking to people at events and parties, because I'm painfully shy."

"What are your thoughts when you are at a party?" I asked. "For example, if you have a hard time making friends, your inner dialog might be: 'This is so awkward. I feel shy. I am afraid. I want to stay out of the spotlight.' What do you say to yourself?"

He said, "All of those things."

I asked, "Have you ever taken classes on how to make friends or maybe a communications course to get over your social awkwardness?"

"No!"

"How about practicing with a friend on dialog and conversation cues to use at a party?"

"No again," he replied. "All I do is tell myself that I am not good enough, and then I leave the party."

Then I asked him what he could do to practice becoming a better communicator.

He said, "Take classes and practice, like I do with my art?"

"Exactly!" I said.

So, what are the areas of your life that you are not successful in? What negative thoughts or words do you use to describe your experience to yourself when you are in those situations? Write them down. Once you have noticed what you are not good at, write down a formula to change that. Use the same technique you use in the areas where you are successful. There are certain things you do to create that success. Once you know what that success formula is, all you need to do is take action on a daily basis to improve any area of your life. However, you must also check in with your inner child to make sure he or she feels safe enough to allow the new successes to come in. That brings us to Step 3.

Part 3: Let's get in touch with that inner child. You are going to start developing a relationship with that child. Become the parent or mentor you wish you could have had in childhood, so your inner child can learn to love him or herself. Eventually that child will grow up and become one with you. The things that used to trigger and set him or her off will no longer have hold over you because you will both feel safe and secure. That's the calm, assertive energy Cesar Millan talks about.

As soon as you wake up in the morning, the first thing you're going to do is ask your inner child, "What do you need?" Then your job is to sit back and listen. When you listen to your inner child, they will tell you what they want. It will usually be self-care related and something simple like, "I want to dance," or "I want to slow down," or "I want to be in nature and play at the beach." When you begin to listen to that child, your whole world will change for the better.

Think about it. When somebody listens to you fully, what happens? Not only do you feel loved, you feel understood. Your inner child is no different and has been trying to get your attention for a very long time. The last piece of this exercise is: whatever that child wants, give it to them. When you do that, you create a structured and safe environment for the child to grow. When that child grows, eventually he or she will become one with you. Then your outer world will begin to change because your inner world will have been healed. I have done this for myself and thousands of my clients. It truly works. That child was open and available. That's when he/she got hurt.

Well, now you are going to set the boundaries that child needs to be free enough to play and yet still have a safe environment to grow. Once you do this, all you need is to maintain that positive energy.

CHAPTER IX
Creating A Healthy Relationship With Food

*"If we could give every individual the right amount
of nourishment and exercise, not too little and not too
much, we would have found the safest way to health."*

—Hippocrates

Part I: Creating A Healthy Relationship With Food

Nutrition can be a tricky subject. As Hippocrates wisely noted, there are "individual needs" to be considered and understood. I find many of my clients have tried everything possible. They tell me: "I work out, I meditate, but for some reason, I can't get my food under control, and I keep going back to my old behaviors. Why do I keep sabotaging my success?" Yet my belief is that it's a mindset, a Belief System, as we have been discussing throughout this book. In order to change our old habits, we need to ditch that Belief System and create a new one. I call this a mindset shift. But how do we do that when it comes to the very thing that has been taking us out of our program? First, we examine our connection to food. Once we determine what that is, we uncover the obstacles that stand in the way of having a truly healthy relationship. Finally, we find solutions to help keep us on track. Once we discover what we need in order to heal, only then can we implement a healthy food plan.

First, how can we define a healthy relationship with food? Sondra Kronberg, MS, RD, CDN, CEDRO, an expert on the treatment of eating disorders, has this to say:

"Forming a healthy relationship with food takes conscious effort, but it is possible. This relationship includes relaxed eating, and practicing balance and flexibility in your eating. These principles will let you feel more at peace with food, as well as help you recognize and stop unhealthy habits."

So, let me ask you: how would you describe your connection to food? If you're anything like I was in the past, I would go for foods that hurt me. They definitely were not healthy or full(filling). I notice that most of my clients have had the same experience. Additionally, we found that their relationship to food was like their relationship with people; a momentary comfort, but not fulfilling. So, my question to you is, if you do this, why do you turn to unhealthy foods for *comfort* knowing they will only cause you to feel worse after? Do they fill an emotional need and provide temporary satisfaction? Think about your eating habits and write down what you discover about yourself.

Stress eating is another contributor to falling off track. Is there too much on your plate, figuratively and literally? Do you have too much responsibility on your shoulders at work or home? Stress can be the barrier that causes us to turn to foods that bring momentary comfort and relief, like a cozy, warm blanket. However, that relief is only temporary and can take you out of your program. Another reason may be monetary concerns, where you think eating healthy costs too much. It could be you feel you lack the time to prepare healthy foods, or that less healthy foods taste great and you don't want to let them go.

Friends and family can be triggers that take us off our healthy eating program. Grandma makes a big meal and insists that you eat it. If you don't, she gets upset and guilt trips you for disrespecting her. Now the whole family is not talking to you. Religion can also be associated with food, and if you don't eat the sacred foods, you could be criticized, so we need to plan for that as well. In many cultures, food is love. When I'm training someone from a different country, I like to get to know their religion, their food, and their culture to help them easily integrate their culture and traditional foods into their program.

Like family, friends can also question changes in our eating habits. When we begin to change, they will often become angry at us. They say things such as, "I liked you better the way you were." They may even end the friendship because you changed. Don't worry—like the Katie Perry song, when one door closes, another opens right away, and you want friends who support and respect the healthy changes you are making.

Many times, what takes people off track is lack of planning. I hear, "I'm so tired, I just want to relax when I get home." I know you're tired. I get tired, too. But it's really important to plan your meals because your tired mind can trick you. It says, "I'll just go to the restaurant, eat something there, and plan tomorrow." However, tomorrow comes and goes and still the same behavior persists. We get famished, and even if the restaurant has healthy food, we go for the menu items we think will fill us up faster. Because of this, when we get knocked off our program, it's hard to get back on. The vicious cycle continues, and even if we have good intentions, we will wake up late and start the vicious cycle over again.

Whatever the triggers are for you, find them and write them down so we can address them in the solutions below.

Triggers and Solutions: Now that we've addressed several obstacles that may stand in the way of your success, below is a blueprint to help you deal with triggers before they come up. They are super simple yet effective solutions to help you stay on track.

Plan Your Meals: I used to ask myself, "How am I going to fit my workout program, my self-care program, into my busy life?" Now, I ask myself, "How am I going to fit my busy life into my self-care plan?" I have learned that if I do not have that solid self-care foundation, I'm not going to be able to sustain my big, fast-paced lifestyle. Creating a self-care plan that includes your meal planning will help you stay on track and will save you time and energy. You won't waste time wondering what you need to do next—such as carving out time to sit down and eat meals when you're hungry. You'd be surprised how many of my clients eat standing up on the go, or even in the car. The body can't digest food properly if you're running down the street while eating it! It's the little important things, like planning, that help you stay on your program. We will discuss more about planning and goal setting in the next couple of chapters. This will give you a blueprint to show you exactly how to do this, so you don't have to think too hard about it.

Deal with your Big Ass Emotions immediately: Stress and Big Ass Emotions will take you off track, and if not addressed, can make you miserable by taking you out of the game of life. When we allow ourselves to feel and work through all of our emotions, they stop stalking us. Remember, emotions are energy. If you feel them, they will disappear and go away. For those of you who are afraid of Big Ass Emotions, have you watched a child move through their emotions? One minute they are up, the next minute they are mad, and a minute later they're happy again. Children can move through every spectrum of the emotional scale within five minutes. They feel them, then they forget about them. It's when we suppress those Big Ass Emotions that they grow bigger and take control of us. We think that, as adults, we're not supposed to be having big emotions, but we do. The key is to feel them and not attach big meaning to them. The solution is that when you become triggered, immediately grab a pen—instead of a cookie or bag of chips—and re-read the chapter about Unpacking Beliefs. This will help you move through those Big Ass Emotions. Remember, if it's hysterical, it's historical. When you write your feelings out, it gives you an outlet, a release, so those emotions will no longer have any power over you. When you do this, nine times out of ten, you'll no longer want those foods that take you off your program.

Practice Self-Care: This is another BIG solution. If you're feeling burned out and stressed, take an Epsom salt bath. Go for a walk out in nature. Instead of picking up that chocolate cake, pick up the phone! Call a friend and say, "I'm getting ready to eat this whole cake, can you please talk me off this ledge?"

Use Journaling to Discover and Learn: I always suggest to my clients, if you want that cake, that's totally fine, you can have it. All I want you to do is journal a whole page about why you want it. Chances are you won't want to eat that cake after you've tried to explain to yourself why you need it. If you are wondering how journaling can help you *not* eat, here's a story.

Jonah.

Jonah, a client, once asked me, "Why do I have to write things out. What is that going to do?"

I said to him, "What do you do for a living?"

He said, "I'm a mortgage broker."

"So, you write contracts for a living, yes?"

He said, "Oh, yeah."

I said, "Let's say I'm buying a house from you. I give you the down payment, and then I am done, yes?"

"No!" he said, "You have to fill out and sign the paper work."

"Why do I have to fill out the paperwork?"

He said, "Because it seals the deal. It makes it legal."

I said, "So, If I didn't fill out that paperwork, it wouldn't be legal then?"

He said, "No, it would not be legal."

I said, "Exactly! Journaling is no different, it helps you seal the deal in your unconscious mind."

And that is why journaling is very important.

<u>Drink Water</u>: This is super important to your plan. Many people are not really hungry when they eat, they just think they are because they are dehydrated. Also, if you drink 8 to 16 oz. of water ten minutes before a meal, it will aid in digestion and help fill you up.

<u>Serve Others</u>: There are times when we're deeply focused on what we are doing. Because of that, our world becomes very small. We tend to be hyper-focused on the little details of our life. It's like having an amazing new Armani suit that has a tiny little ink stain on it. The entire suit is perfect except for this one tiny little spot. However, that spot is the only thing we can think about. Being of service helps us get our head out of our butt and gives us a broader perspective on our life. The service doesn't have to be big either. A simple compliment. Holding the door open for someone. Little acts of kindness like that allow us to brighten someone's day and shift our hyper-focused mindset away from our own problems. When you think about being of service to someone else, you don't think about your problems, and the change of perspective can sometimes even help you solve them!

So, there you have it. Simple solutions to simple triggers that used to take you out of the game and sabotage your program. In the next section, I will share with you the eight foods most likely to cause inflammation in your body, and then show you which healthy foods you can add to your food plan to ensure your ultimate results—so we can build you a rocket ship to get you to the moon!

Part II: The Eight Most Inflammatory Foods

Before we get started, I want to talk about why nutrition is so important. There's a documentary called *The Magic Pill* which explains how our society has been trained to reach outside of ourselves and take pills to fix our problems. But of course, no magic pill is going to fix your life. Believe me, if it were out there, I would have found it. I have searched for magic pills in my own life and in my work with many different types of people, from multi-billionaires to foster children. I remember working with my friend who ran several foster homes. Many of her foster children had mental illnesses like schizophrenia, borderline personality, and cognitive disabilities like anxiety and PTSD. Needless to say, they had a lot of big emotions and used pills to try and calm those emotions down. But, as we discussed earlier in this book, when a living being doesn't receive the proper exercise, structure, nutrition, and purpose, no matter how many drugs or pills they take, it will not work.

Instead, we changed the children's nutrition, had them meditate, and helped them come up with their own life purpose. In addition, I facilitated their exercise program. Working with my beautiful foster children wasn't easy, and there was a major BS resistance. However, 90% of those children were able to stop 100% of their medications. Only a few with more severe mental illnesses needed medication, and they were able to reduce their medication drastically. In that process, I discovered what an important role food plays, not only in our physical health, but in our mental health as well.

In the previous section of this chapter, we talked about our relationship to food, what was blocking us from success in our program, and solutions that might eliminate those blocks. Now, we're going to talk about the eight top foods that cause inflammation in the body, and what to do about them, so you can reduce inflammation and lose weight. Our society has been led to believe that if a package says "organic" on it, it must be good for you, but that's not the case at all. Many of those "healthy" foods are the very reason you're overweight, gaining weight, or inflamed. Clients say to me, "Kim, I'm eating perfectly, but I'm still overweight no matter what I do. It's probably the way I'm made. Someone like me isn't meant to be lean." I call BS on that! We will now debunk the "Healthy Organic Myth" and show you the eight most inflammatory foods. Then we're going to discuss the foods you will love that improve lifestyle, mindset, and body.

Mary.

I had a client named Mary who worked out two to three days per week with me, and two days on her own. She followed her exercise program exactly the way I had asked her to. However, she was gaining weight and becoming bloated.

She kept telling me, "Kim, it's the workouts. My body doesn't like what we're doing."

I told her, "It's not the workouts, trust me."

She argued and told me she felt discouraged.

I said, "Look at your joints, your wrists, elbows, and ankles. See how bloated they are? What that's telling me is that your body is inflamed, and more than likely, it's caused from a food allergy. Give me at least a week where you follow an anti-inflammatory food diet. If you're still feeling bloated, we'll change up your workouts and try another approach."

She agreed and kept a journal to record every piece of food that passed her lips.

After three days of journaling, she came to me and said, "See, Kim, I'm eating perfectly. There's no reason why I should be gaining weight and getting puffy."

She handed me her journal, and my jaw hit the floor.

I said, "Oh my gosh, I know exactly why you're becoming bloated. Your entire diet is filled with foods that are causing inflammation in your body, even though they say they're healthy and organic. Here's what I want you to do. For just one week, take these eight inflammatory foods out of your diet and let's see what happens."

She complied, and within one week she lost 5lbs., her bloating went away, and her vitality came back. She felt so good she decided she wanted to continue eating this way. Within 28 days, she had achieved her goal weight, her joints were no longer sore, she wasn't exhausted after her workouts, and she took her workouts to a whole new level.

Those foods were draining her of her precious energy, and they're probably doing the same to you. So, what we're going to do is educate you on the eight most inflammatory foods that drain your brain and body. Then we'll talk about the foods that will provide you with the life force you are looking for.

Here are the eight most inflammatory foods:

Inflammatory Food #1—Wheat/Gluten: The number one inflammatory food you want to stay away from is wheat, specifically gluten. According to Dr. William Davis, the author of *Wheat Belly*, gluten is a protein composite found in several types of grains, including wheat, spelt, rye and barley. When gluten reaches the digestive tract and is exposed to the cells of the immune system, those cells mistakenly believe it is coming from some sort of foreign invader, like bacteria. In certain people who are sensitive to gluten, this causes the immune system to mount an attack against it. Because of this, many people are suffering from intense weight gain, digestive disorders, and even autoimmune disorders.

Inflammatory Food #2—Dairy: According to HealthLine. com, cow's milk has a higher amount of lactose than milk from other animals, and up to 75 % of the world's population has some form of lactose intolerance. In addition, many milks have extra hormones pumped into them. Drinking these antibiotics and steroids can cause allergic reactions in the body, causing it to become inflamed. Yet, there are wonderful benefits from drinking milk as well. If you will not take dairy out of your diet, try Grass Fed, antibiotic-free A2 milk. It's been proven to digest better in the body. You can also try goat's milk. Think about it. A cow has four stomachs. A goat's body has properties more like humans and only has one stomach. Therefore, their milk is easier to digest.

Inflammatory Food #3—Refined Sugar: Have you ever noticed you may experience a high directly after eating sugar and then a crash soon after? This reaction is especially noticeable in kids. Give a kid a candy bar and watch him go. They will literally bounce off the walls. However, once that sugar high has worn off, they are nodding off like a heroin addict. Studies have shown that sugar, especially refined sugar, taps into the same pleasure center in the brain as cocaine. Researchers have found that sugar is even more addictive than cocaine. Producers of sugary foods and beverages know this and will put it in just about everything to ensure we keep consuming their products. It's sad to me, especially when my daughter constantly cries for cookies, candy, and cakes when we are at the grocery store. It's hard to say no; she doesn't understand why she can't have it all the time.

Inflammatory Food #4—Conventional Meats: Remember, you are what you eat. You are also consuming what the animal has been eating, so when farmers pump animals full of testosterone and antibiotics, you are ingesting those chemicals as well. Processed meats such as bacon, sausages, and ham can cause cancer, according to the World Health Organization (WHO). They reported that 50g of processed meat a day—less than two slices of bacon—increased the chances of developing colorectal cancer by 18%. In addition, these processed animal products we consume do not have the nutrients they once did. Try an experiment. Pick up an organic brown egg and a non-organic white egg and squeeze them with your fingers. Notice the organic brown egg is harder to break then the non-organic white egg. The same goes for a chicken bone. Notice that, if you have a non-organic chicken bone, it's easier to break then an organic chicken bone. There's a reason for that. I was chatting with a doctor friend of mine. He said he is seeing more broken bones in children than 20 years ago. Children's bones are not as strong because the food they are consuming is not as nutritious as it once was.

Inflammatory Food #5—Soy: Now, if the soy is organic and in its natural form, I say go for it. However, 90% of our soy is genetically modified, and we're putting it in everything. I remember reading an article by Dr. Josh Axe, who explained that soy is being put in baby formula, and that in its refined state, it raises estrogen levels. That causes more cases of breast cancer and other problems, so be mindful of the type of soy you're putting into your body. Make sure it has the label, Non-GMO, and is also organic.

Inflammatory Food #6—Corn: Beware of processed corn and HFCS (high fructose corn syrups). According to Sylvie Tremblay, MSC, "While unprocessed corn is healthy in moderation, you should avoid processed corn products. Corn is one of the cheapest sources of sugar in the United States, thanks to agricultural policies that subsidize corn crops, so food manufacturers often turn to high-fructose corn syrup, or HFCS, as a low-cost sweetener for processed foods. HFCS has no place in a diet. According to research conducted at Princeton University, consuming HFCS over the table sugar makes weight gain and chronic diseases, like diabetes, more likely."

My clients say to me, "Kim, what about my corn chips? I can't eat my chips?" I say, "Think about it. With 99% of our corn being genetically modified, what if it causes a mutation of cells in your body?" Our bodies do not like this GMO corn that is being modified by man. It does not do well in the body. That being said, if you go and get 100% organic blue chips, those could be okay, but only in moderation. Otherwise, stay away from corn, especially processed corn. The body does better when you avoid grains altogether. When grains are avoided, the body manages digestion more easily.

Inflammatory Food #7—Vegetable Oils: You know, my grandma used to think she was doing a good thing by frying everything in vegetable oil. She thought it was all about vegetables, and really it was the worst kind of oil she could have used. It's very important to use other kinds of oils. Vegetable oils include canola oil and corn oil. These oils can cause havoc in the body and can result in allergic reactions. Vegetable oils can damage your immune system. According Robin Konie, RSMT, CLMA, vegetable oils are bad because they contain very high levels of polyunsaturated fats (PUFAs).

The fat content of the human body is about 97% *saturated* and *monounsaturated* fat. Our body needs fat for rebuilding cells and for hormone production, but it can only use what we give it. Polyunsaturated fats are a problem because they are highly unstable. They oxidize easily. These oxidized fats can cause inflammation and mutation in cells. That oxidation is linked to all sorts of issues, including cancer, heart disease, and endometriosis. PUFAs are bad news.

Inflammatory Food #8—Alcohol: You may be saying, "Now, Kim, you had me at hello with all the inflammatory foods. However, I refuse to let go of my alcohol completely." I get it. I'm not saying give up alcohol, but drink it in moderation because, when you are drinking alcohol, digestion stops. Your body works only on getting rid of the toxins the alcohol is creating. For example, have you ever noticed someone at the gym who obviously went on a drinking binge the night before? What do they smell like? Alcohol. Why? When they sweat, the alcohol oozes out through their pores, and it doesn't smell good. There's a reason for the foul smell. Alcohol is highly toxic, and the body is trying to eliminate it. Therefore, be mindful of how much you drink. Additionally, what happens when we drink is that the body raises estrogen levels. This will cause your joints to become inflamed, which in turn causes your body to hold on to water, and you will become bloated. According to the National Institute of Alcohol Abuse and Alcoholism (niaaa. nih.gov), in addition to causing you to gain weight, overconsumption of alcohol can cause a myriad of ailments.

Part III: The Eight Top Foods That Will Help Your Body Thrive

> *"The doctor of the future will no longer treat the human frame with drugs, but rather will cure and prevent disease with nutrition."*
> —Thomas Edison

Now let's talk about the eight foods that help provide an alkaline body.

Good Food #1—Dark Leafy Greens: These include kale, collard greens, spinach, and cruciferous vegetables like broccoli and brussels sprouts. These are all wonderful foods for us to eat. They are also cancer fighting agents. Leafy greens, especially dark greens, are a great source of vitamins A, C, and K, and are traditionally a good source of calcium and iron and are packed with fiber.

Good Food #2—Humanely Raised Proteins: These include protein from grass-fed cows, free-ranch organic chickens that have been fed worms instead of corn, and wild-caught Alaskan fish like salmon, which has omega-3's that help reduce inflammation in the body. Studies have shown that consumption of omega-3's is linked to having healthy brain function. Vitamin B12—which helps your body produce red blood cells and DNA, supports your immune system, and encourages healthy nerve function—is found naturally only in animal sources. That means people who don't eat meat or dairy can have trouble reaching the daily recommended doses.

Good Food #3—Bone Broth: Bone broth is very soothing to the gut. Many people have a fast-paced, stressful lifestyle. Many have a condition called leaky gut. Some of the benefits of bone broth are that it will help heal the lining of your stomach, improve digestion, enhance your immune system, and help bones grow. Among the nutrients in bone broth are collagen and chondroitin, which construct cartilage. When you introduce these substances to the body, your joints can heal. Collagen is a protein your body uses extensively to keep your skin healthy. Without it, our skin would gradually lose elasticity and its healthy color, causing us to age quickly. Glutathione is another vitamin in bone broth which helps the body regenerate new tissue.

Good Food #4—Dark Berries: Blueberries, strawberries, raspberries, and blackberries have nutritious antioxidants that help heal the body. They also help with brain function. These are wonderful foods that have cancer-fighting properties.

Good Food #5—Flax Seeds: Flaxseeds are small, brown, tan or golden-colored seeds. They are the richest source of the omega-3 fatty acids called alpha-linolenic acids. Several studies have found that flaxseed has the potential to reduce the risk of heart disease, cancer, stroke and diabetes. It can also improve digestion, complexion, cholesterol levels, and hormone levels. They're a wonderful source of fiber and aid in elimination, and your elimination is the key to your health; flax seeds are helpful in cleansing the colon. Dr. Bob Rakowski, a near and dear friend of mine and also the best naturopathic doctor known to human-kind, always reminds me of the seven ways to check whether we are healthy. He states that you should eat right, sleep right, talk right, think right, drink right, move right, and "poop right" every single day (I love when he says this!). So, flaxseeds are one thing you can con-sume in order to create a healthy intestinal tract.

Good Food #6—Healthy Fats: Coconut oil, grass-fed ghee butter, avocado oils, olive oils, and nuts are all very good sources of healthy fat. Many people think that fat is bad. I'm here to de-bunk the fat-free craze and say that fat is essential to our health.

Good Food #7—Fermented Foods: Fermented foods, includ-ing sauerkraut, kimchi, and grass-fed kefir. Kefir is a probiotic drink made from milk, so your stomach may not be able to tolerate it, but if you do you drink it, make sure it's from grass-fed cows. These fermented foods provide the body with the most convenient way to obtain a daily dose of beneficial pro-biotic bacteria. Some of the many ways that fermented foods support overall health include aiding in digestion, cognitive function, boosting immunity, healing irritable bowel disease, providing minerals that build bone density, helping fight allergies, and killing harmful yeast and microbes that cause issues like candida.

Good Food #8—Prebiotic Foods: Why prebiotics? They act like a fertilizer and a fiber and create a cleaning agent so good bacteria can grow. Prebiotic foods are garlic, onions; even asparagus, believe it or not, is a wonderful source. Again, putting in healthy fiber, which acts like a fertilizer, allows good bacteria to grow. So, the trick is to get prebiotic *and* probiotic foods into every meal that you have.

"Health is a state of complete harmony of the body, mind and spirit. When one is free from physical disabilities and mental distractions, the gates of the soul open."
–B.K.S. Iyengar

So, there you have it! The eight top foods to help heal the lining of your gut and aid in preventing inflammation in the body. These are great foods to eat to create a balanced mindset. In turn, that's going to create a solid foundation so your body can run beautifully, and when your body runs beautifully, so does everything else. Remember: it all starts with self-care. An important part of self-care is ingesting healthy foods into our bodies to ensure optimal results. In the next chapter we will go over the fabulous five top vitamins to add into your daily life.

CHAPTER X
Five Fabulous Vitamins and Supplements That Heal

"Let food be thy medicine and medicine be thy food."

—Hippocrates

I remember going through one of the roughest times of my life. My body was suffering from many ailments. I didn't know what was happening. All I knew was that my body was failing me. As I explained in previous chapters, I went to several doctors trying to figure out what was wrong with me. Not one could identify the problem, so I saw several naturopathic doctors. They loaded me up with thousands of dollars' worth of vitamins, which made my liver enzymes skyrocket. After all of this, I contacted my friend, Dr. Bob Rakowski. I love this man and have known him and his family for over 20 years, so I knew I could trust him. Don't ask me why I didn't talk to him sooner. He said, "Kim, all of these doctors, even the natural docs, make their money from loading you up on pills, and frankly, you don't need all of that. Just take these five fabulous supplements and call it a day."

I couldn't believe it. After tens of thousands of dollars thrown into the abyss of the medical machine, my recovery was made possible by: taking a few vitamins; eating healthy, non-inflammatory foods; exercising moderately; and meditating! If I had only known this from the beginning, I would have saved many sleepless nights and tons of money.

Vitamins are good in moderation, and you want to make sure you are purchasing superb quality. Many worthless versions of vitamins have fillers in them, and they do nothing. The rule of thumb is DO NOT buy your vitamins from Trader Joe's, GNC, Costco, Rite Aid, CVS or a store equivalent to these. Brand names you can trust are Metagenics, Standard Process, and New Chapter. Whole Foods and Sprouts also have great quality, if you have them in your area.

Here are the Fab Five vitamins and supplements you should add to your daily plan:

#1—Multivitamins: Multivitamins are a good supplement for those who don't always have time to shop for fresh vegetables, fruits, and whole grains. But most health experts agree that a multivitamin is no replacement for a good, well-balanced diet.

#2—Greens: Many people do not include enough greens in their diet. As a matter fact, if we were to eat the amount of greens we needed; it would equal about fourteen servings. If you're like me, that's too much to eat in a day, but a scoop of good quality green powder will do wonders. What greens do is create alkalinity in the body. When the body is alkaline, disease cannot grow. But again, you want to create a good green formula to put into your morning shake or into a bone broth protein shake. I find Dr. Axe's Bone Broth Protein agrees with my body. Nutragen has a vegan source of protein. With a scoop of greens, you can have a well-balanced morning shake to aid in keeping your body balanced. Recommended daily intake (RDI) differs for each supplement of greens. Read the label and take the suggested amount.

#3—Pre and Probiotics: Many people know about the benefits of probiotics, which are friendly bacteria that can improve your health by keeping your body balanced. Good sources of probiotics include yogurt, kefir, sauerkraut, and kimchi. Even pickles are a great source. What most people do not know, however, is that we need prebiotics to create fertilizer so the probiotics can grow. Prebiotics are types of dietary fiber that feed the friendly bacteria in your gut. This helps produce nutrients for your colon cells, which leads to a healthier digestive system. The most popular prebiotics include garlic, onions, asparagus, chicory root, artichokes, dandelion greens, and bananas, to name a few. The RDI should provide at least 1 billion CFUs (colony forming units, i.e., viable cells), with doses typically ranging between 1 billion and 10 billion CFUs daily for adults. The RDI is a minimum of 5 grams of prebiotics a day.

#4—Magnesium: Magnesium is an essential mineral nutrient that helps calm the body and the brain. It also aids in elimination and promotes sleep, so it's a beautiful way to calm down the body naturally. Magnesium can be found in dark chocolate, avocados, nuts, legumes, and tofu, but many people don't reach the recommended daily intake (RDI) of 400 mg.

#5—Omega-3: Omega-3s are healthy fats that help prevent inflammation in the body, especially in the brain. They also help prevent inflammation in the gut. Many people ingest too many of the less healthy Omega-6 fats. Our bodies tend to be stressed out and super inflamed, but Omega-3s help calm that down and help with the release of toxins in the body. You can receive high amounts of Omega-3 fats from fatty fish like salmon and mackerel. You can also find Omega-3s in walnuts, flax seeds, and chia seeds. The recommended daily intake (RDI) is 250–500 mg of Omega-3s per day for healthy adults.

So, there you have it. These Fab Five nutrients have worked wonders for me and they can for you, too. Remember that many naturalistic doctors will try to push vitamins on you. You don't need all of that. Simply focus on the Fab Five and fuel your rocket ship to blast you to the moon!

CHAPTER XI
Busting Through Weight-loss Plateaus

*"All parts of the body which have a function, if used
in moderation and exercised in labors in which each
is accustomed, become thereby healthy, well developed,
and age more slowly, but if unused they become liable to
disease, defective in growth, and age quickly."*
—Hippocrates

Have you ever noticed how much energy dogs have? Let's say
I have a chihuahua, and I don't exercise him. I do not provide
structure or purpose. What do you think that dog is going to
do to my couch if I leave him locked up in a room all day? He's
going to chew it apart! What do you think is going to happen
to that dog's mental state? He might become anxious, insecure,
develop some sort of neurosis or fixations (addiction, in human
terms) to deal with all that pent-up energy.

Humans are no different. We, too, need to have our energy
directed in a healthy way. As humans, we live in a constant
state of fight, freeze, or flight. We get stuck in survival mode.
Humans become burnt out from having too much stress in
their lives, and at the rate they go, they will not be able to
sustain their lifestyles for long. So, they tell themselves, "Okay!
I'm going to start an exercise program." They work out super
hard, and what happens? They quit or, worse, they get injured.
Or they may hire a personal trainer who shames and punishes
them for not working hard enough.

Unfortunately, programs haven't trained our personal trainers to look out for adrenal fatigue or burnout. These well-meaning trainers have been conditioned by society that "no pain is no gain," and that you always have to work harder and do more. As for me, I am a whole other kind of trainer. My guess is that if you are reading this book, you and your body are already burned out. The last thing you need is a kick-your-butt program. However, even though mine is not a kick-your-butt program, it will still give you the results you are looking for. I always tell my clients, "Less is more!"

So, let me ask you: have you ever been on a weight loss and fitness program? If so, you were probably very excited starting out. You joined a gym, bought some sexy workout clothes, cleaned out your pantry and refrigerator, and dumped your junk food stash. You were ready to go, and in about two weeks—give or take a few days—something happened; you decided to quit. Why?

Many people find change scary, even if it is positive change. Even losing weight can be scary, if you are afraid of change. Ask yourself what change means to you. My program will assist you in getting clear about what it is you actually want to change, how to make that change fun by keeping it exciting, and most importantly, how to make it last. Having taught Emotional Fitness for over two decades, I have seen people set unrealistic and unhealthy goals for themselves. They came to realize that what they thought they wanted was very different from what they were ready to create for themselves. In addition, many new clients come to me already burned out. The last thing they need is a kick-your-butt kind of program. If these people continue to push themselves, they will eventually get injured and their body will force them to quit because, again, they are already burned out and have nothing left to give. The people who come to me for help are usually at the end of their rope and need a little guidance to help them face the truth without making themselves wrong. In this new decision, they finally have the security and support to face those inner demons and defeat them.

In this chapter, I will assist you to become clear while designing a custom program to meet your particular needs. It will take you less than one hour a day. Lastly, you will learn to integrate your goals into your daily life, ensuring results that last. If you feel like you want or need more guidance, I have created a Video Workout Series titled, Repair—Rebuild—Recover, which is an accelerated program that my A-List celebrities use. It will help you transform your body in about 120 Days.

Mind & Body Transformation Made Easy: Learn to Have Fun Through Fitness!

Have you ever needed to exercise but couldn't get yourself to take the first step, even though you knew it would be good for you? Have you ever gotten a sick feeling in your stomach while looking in the mirror because you knew you needed to make a change but didn't know how? Or maybe you simply didn't want to. Why is exercise so painful to most of us, even though we know it's good for us? These are questions and experiences that I have had myself.

I was quite plump when I was younger. Later, I had personal trainers and coaches to help me lose weight, enter fitness competitions, and become a fitness model. I did quite well. However, when all was said and done and the competitions were over, I couldn't get myself to exercise anymore. I just didn't want to; I was like a stubborn mule. My energy level dropped seriously, and anxiety began to consume my life. Whenever I thought about exercising, I would get a sick feeling in my stomach. The pain at the thought of spending hours in the gym overrode the anxiety I was experiencing over my physical condition. I was stuck and had to find a way out. However, after I figured out how to add fitness into my life and have fun again, I became pregnant which took me through another loop because now my body wasn't able to move the way it did in the past.

Not only did I have to relearn how to exercise, I had the added pressure of hormones, which I also had to manage.

As a result, I created "Kimberly Lou: Repair—Rebuild—Recover," a unique Three Phase Emotional Fitness Series consisting of three progressively challenging systems. Each system has a rotating focus on: Re-patterning the way your body moves; Building Strength, Balance, and Coordination; and Shedding Excess Weight with Advanced Training to Achieve Optimal Fitness. All three levels keep your mind and body stimulated while you achieve advanced levels of fitness.

Part I – Appreciate Yourself and Keep Moving!

Have you ever known someone who was never satisfied, and no matter how much you did for them it was never enough? How did it make you feel? It probably didn't make you feel good at all. Most people have a tendency to treat themselves and their bodies harshly, whether physically or through negative thinking. However, while training clients, I have them say out loud what they appreciate about themselves and their bodies. I will use my client, Jenny, as an example.

Jenny.

Jenny weighed over 300 pounds, and every time she went to exercise, it was especially hard for her because she was carrying so much weight. It was too painful on her ankles and joints, or at least that's the excuse she was using at the time. She didn't realize her thoughts had a lot more to do with how she was feeling than her physical condition did.

While training with Jenny, I listened to her tone of voice and the harsh criticism she used on herself. When she spoke about her body, it was with such disgust that I could see why she was so tired all the time. With the amount of negative energy her thoughts were sending through her body, she could have destroyed a planet.

One day, while training, I told her that she was going to climb up a nearby hill, but before she even started, she had quit. She was already telling herself she couldn't do it. In the middle of our training session, she had a meltdown and refused to budge. Then she started having pain all over her body. What she didn't realize was that her brain was trying to trick her into stopping. It was like one of those out-of-control psycho kids you see on The Super Nanny show, throwing a tantrum when they don't get their way. Or, better yet, like The Exorcist movie where the child is possessed, and her head is spinning around in circles, eyes bulging out of their sockets. Jenny's body was possessed by a mind that didn't believe in her own ability or in the inner strength she shares with all of humanity.

What her ego didn't realize (the part of her doing all the talking) was that I knew all of its tricks. I told Jenny to keep moving and send love to her body.

"What do you mean send love to my body?" she said. "That's ridiculous!"

"Do it!" I said, not taking no for an answer.

With every little step Jenny took, she would say, "I love you, legs!...I love you, feet!...I love you, lungs!...I love you, heart!" With each step, she became stronger and stronger. By the time she climbed to the top of the hill, her ankles and feet had stopped hurting, and she had so much energy that she wanted to keep going.

Note: When you can appreciate yourself and lighten up physically and emotionally, your body will start to respond positively, resulting in less injury and overall better health. Appreciate yourself and keep moving!

Part II - Focus on What Is Working

On occasion, I have been fortunate enough to work with professional athletes. Sometimes, they have come to me with injuries. One of my clients, Kevin, a former NBA player, came to me with a ruptured Achilles tendon and had to have surgery. The doctors told him he would be in a cast for at least six to eight weeks, and that he would have to walk with a boot for another six to nine months. For the very active man that he is, this was not good news.

Kevin had a very strong mind. He was adamant about not taking any painkillers or drugs during his recovery. The doctors said they didn't want him using his foot at all during that time, but that didn't sound right to me. After discussing his situation with my good friend, Dr. Robert Rakowski from Natural Medicine Center in Houston, I felt confident taking my client's training to the next level. During our training session, I had him work the leg that was not in a cast. Simultaneously, I had him visualize working the leg that had the cast on it.

Notice I didn't say the "good leg" or "bad leg." I wanted to get away from focusing on words like "good" and "bad." Words are very powerful. I remember I used to say things like "killing two birds with one stone," until I actually killed two doves standing in the middle of the street. They didn't move. I'm trying to blame the birds because I was devastated. Feathers flew up every which way. I had actually killed two birds with one stone... Firestone tire, that is. I became very careful with my words after that day.

Sometimes, Kevin made reference to his "good" or "bad" leg, and I would correct him immediately, encouraging him to focus on the working leg and have him visualize the leg in the cast being healed. I had him imagine performing the exercise with the leg in the cast at the same time. Remember, if you can see it, you can achieve it. Your body responds to the signals your mind sends to it. Pretty soon, he was out of his cast without using any drugs, and all within four weeks. After only three months, he was walking without his booty.

While I would like to take credit for this, he actually did most of the work—using his mind. I just helped him tweak his thinking a little bit and encouraged him to do what he and his body already knew how to do.

Proverb: In the most painful times in our lives, we tend to focus on the pain, when in actuality, this is the time to focus on what's working. The pain is information to teach you something. So, what are you going to learn from it? Focus on what's working!

Part III – Now Let's Get Moving: Hit It and Quit It!

When you begin to add fitness to your daily routine, whether you exercise inside or out, the results will be the same. I recommend mixing it up! Most of my clients work out in a gym, so I've put together this fitness routine based on training inside the gym. I would also like to mention that exercising outside has so many benefits. First of all, you're not confined to a room and a roof. The sky is the limit, baby. When you go outside, you connect to nature. Your body is back in its natural habitat. Going to a park or someplace with trees can be invigorating.

Here are a few ideas on how to exercise outside: A park bench can be a perfect jungle gym. You can do pushups, lunges, triceps dips, and core exercises. In addition, if you want some resistance, buy a $7 exercise band at your local Target or Wal-Mart; you can purchase a set of three for as little as $15.00 and take them with you for your outside workouts, or when you travel. It's really about giving yourself some options. You don't want to get to a place where you are denying yourself the benefits of working out just because the gym is closed or you are traveling with no gym in sight. Learn to be flexible and you may find yourself exercising on a beach, in a park or schoolyard, on a mountain, in a meadow, or by a river or stream. The possibilities are endless if you let them be.

Most people think that they have to work out for hours and hours to have a "Perfect Body." Here is a way for you to get in and out of the gym in less than an hour. Most of my clients are in and out within 45 minutes. We begin with five minutes of meditation and visualization. Next, we spend

15 minutes performing reconstructive exercises and myofascial release. Then we perform 30 minutes of exercise with weights and cardio. The last five minutes is for stretching. Here is the Repair—Rebuild—Recover four-step program that will get you in and out of the gym in less than an hour while having fun doing it.

Repair—Rebuild—Recover: Four Steps to Get In and Out of the Gym in Half The Time

We all face the challenge of finding time and motivation for our exercise program. I have been in the fitness and wellness industry for over 20 years. To keep things exciting, I've had to find some very creative ways to make exercise fun. I have hit highs and lows in my routine, and I've had my share of success and challenges. There have been times when I have flat-out resisted exercise, even though I knew it would be good for me. To help get me through those times, I created a four-step program to help me get in and out of the gym in half the time, and to assist me in breaking through some tough mental barriers.

Step I—Visualization and Meditation (approximately 5 minutes): It's a fact that if you can see it, you can achieve it. I have experienced this in my own life, and I've had the pleasure of training many athletes. Not surprisingly, the athletes who have incorporated visualization techniques in reaching their goals have far surpassed the ones who didn't. I will use my good friend, Carrie, as an example.

Carrie.

Carrie came to me because she was trying to determine whether or not to quit her career as a professional beach volleyball player. Even though she loved the sport, she was training over five hours a day and was still placing near the bottom at every tournament. So, each Monday we would meet to work on bettering her mental skills. While this did help, she was still losing.

Then the unspeakable happened; during one of Carrie's practice sessions, she injured her knee. Frustrated and near tears, she called me. That's when I suggested visualization.

That week Carrie visualized the experience of being on the court. She imagined the warm sand between her toes. She felt the ball on her hand as she crushed it over the net. In her mind, she saw her opponent unable to get to the ball. Finally, she saw herself holding the winner's trophy in her hands.

Two weeks later, I got a call from Carrie. Not only did her injury heal, she beat the pants off her competition and won the tournament. After that experience, I knew I would incorporate visualization techniques for all of my clients, whether or not they were professional athletes.

Step II—Working Your Core (20 minutes): Most people begin their workout with cardio.

While better than nothing, it's actually a waste of time because it takes approximately 20 minutes of cardio to start burning fat. For the quickest results, work your core before starting your cardio workout because you will burn sugar for 20 minutes while warming up and preparing your body for the exercise to come.

For now, I must emphasize that myofascial release and reconstructive exercise is the most important thing you can do for your body. It builds stronger, freer muscles, resulting in a more efficient workout. If your muscles are tight and weak, it causes the surrounding muscles to lose strength and become imbalanced, which inevitably causes injury. Myofascial release builds a strong foundation on which a more powerful, vibrant physical experience will be built. Without a solid foundation, the house—no matter how impressive the structure—will not stand. Your body is your house. It's what you live in, and like any house, it has to be built on something solid. A strong core will help you avoid paying a heavy physical price later on.

Judy.

My client, Judy, came to me wanting to lose a couple of pounds for her 80th birthday. But what was most important to Judy was to be able to reach behind her back and unsnap her bra strap without causing pain. Because Judy had tight and weak muscles, they were overcompensating and she was constantly injuring herself, which ultimately resulted in shoulder surgery. Because of her injured shoulder, Judy couldn't raise her arms over her head. After one day of visualizing and performing reconstructive exercises, she was able to lift both arms completely straight, and within one week—which included three sessions—she was able to unhook her bra strap with ease and grace. Success!

I realize the thought of an 80-year old woman unhooking her bra strap may not mean much for a general audience, but there's a group of gentlemen at the senior center that think it's the best news since Medicare. Performing myofascial release and reconstructive exercises to lay a solid foundation helps get the muscles activated and warm, and it prepares you for step three!

Step III – Combining Weight and Cardio Training (approximately 30 minutes): I have learned that, unless you're a professional body builder who wants to gain a boatload of weight, you don't need to rest after each set. Can you imagine doing a set of chest exercises....then resting....then another set....then resting. That is boring! And even though, on the second cycle of your workout program, this type of exercise will be performed, when I stop, I don't want to start again. It takes way too long. And heaven forbid someone tries to strike up a conversation with me, and now I have wasted two hours at the gym and have not even gotten halfway through my routine. If you're anything like me, you have way better things to do with your time than to sit around the gym all day. That's why I incorporate cardio into my weight routine.

Because I start by working reconstructive exercises and myofascial release, I'm already warm and burning fat. I super-set my exercises to cut my workout time in half. If I'm to train my back that day, I will super-set two exercises with back, then immediately grab a jump rope or do something that has to do with cardio, so that I can keep my heart rate up and keep burning. Then I will work an ancillary body part, like biceps or triceps, or perform a core exercise like a plank.

Tip: Incorporate visualization into your routine. When you visualize your desired goal while you train, you forget to complain. When you forget to complain, you actually start having a good time. When you have a good time, time flies and, before you know it, the workout is over. So, you actually get more done in less time on a consistent basis. Of course, once you get used to that, you'll have to give up your seat in Congress!

Now it's time to cool down and prepare your body for step four.

Step IV—Stretching and Recovery (approximately 5 minutes): After every workout, incorporate stretching, meditation, and verbally thanking yourself for a job well done. When you do this, you allow your body time to recover and settle back into its natural groove. By adding breathing and meditation, you will be more balanced. Believe me, your unconscious remembers everything you do and everything you say. If you are straining your body and denying it recovery, it will retaliate and resist you.

Think about it! We all know that people love to be appreciated. When someone appreciates you, it makes you want to do more. Well, your body is no different. Acknowledge yourself for a job well done; you will want to exercise more often, and your body will respond in some amazing ways! Affirm for yourself: "My body is strong, my body is healthy, and I can do anything I set my mind to."

To sum up everything we've looked at:

> Step I: Visualize—What you see you can achieve.
>
> Step II: Myofascial Release and Reconstructive Exercises—Stabilize and strengthen your muscles, freeing them to work more efficiently.
>
> Step III: Combine Weights and Cardio—Incorporate weight training with cardio, saving precious time and energy.
>
> Step IV: Recovery—Stretch, meditate, and verbally thank your body.

So, in less time than it takes to watch the latest episode of *Grey's Anatomy*, you can be doing something great for your own anatomy!

I know we've covered a lot of information. For more tips on how to add a fun program to fit your lifestyle, and if you feel you want or need more guidance, I have created a Video Workout Series, Repair—Rebuild—Recover, which is the accelerated program that my A-List Celebrities use. It will help you transform your body in about 120 Days. Now let's have fun!

A Closing Story About Exercise

Exercise doesn't have to be hard work. Just remember to have fun, and the rest will come without even trying. For those of you who still think that you are too old, too fat, too sick, or too whatever to add fitness into your daily routine, I will close with this story:

Dad.

My father was a very sick man, but he knew, like you do, that it was time he started feeling better. So, he flew me to China, where he had lived for the last twelve years, to come up with a fitness program for him. Knowing my father's condition, I wanted to speak with his doctor before putting him on any kind of program (to make sure I didn't kill him!). My father and I went to one of his dialysis sessions, his home away from home. He did dialysis three days a week. I met with his doctor while we were there.

After about three hours, the doctor came over to me and my father and explained that, not only did my father have diabetes that required him to take insulin every day to live, he also had only 1% function of both of his kidneys. This meant that this man didn't even have the privilege to urinate without being hooked up to a machine to drain his bodily fluids. He also had a condition where his brain was being attacked repeatedly by parasites. But that was not the worst of his condition; the doctor went on to say that my father's heart was failing fast, and that he could pass away at any moment.

The doctor said that every time Dad got onto one of the dialysis machines, he risked heart failure because his heart was too weak to keep up with the machine that cleaned his blood and drained his fluids. As a matter of fact, as he said that, my father's blood pressure dropped, so they had to turn off the machine to let his heart rest. Even after all of that, the doctor still thought it would be beneficial for my father to add fitness to his daily life.

The next day, I created a fitness routine that my father could easily do sitting down. After a month, he was doing his exercises every day to keep a clear mind and his spirits up. So, if my father with diabetes, two failing kidneys, parasites in his brain, and heart disease, can add fitness to his routine, so can you.

CHAPTER XII
Visioning vs. Goal Setting and Mental Imagery

"The only thing worse than being blind is having sight but no vision."

—Helen Keller

Every morning, I condition my brain and body for success. I call it visioning. Visioning will be your best friend. I do this as soon as I wake up in the morning and in the evening when I retire; I am planting seeds of success and planning the vision of what my inner being wants to achieve. I didn't always do this. At the beginning of my inner journey, I spent most my free time at Agape International Spirituality Center.

As you read earlier, I was going through a very rough time, and I didn't know my ass from a hole in the ground. My health was failing me, I was trying to reestablish what I wanted to do with my life, and I was going through my divorce. I felt completely lost because I didn't know who I was, what I wanted or, even if I did know, I didn't think I had the tools to achieve it. I asked Rev. Michael Bernard Beckwith, New Thought minister, author, and founder of the Agape International Spiritual Center in Culver City, about visioning because I didn't understand what he was talking about at first. I would attend his silent meditation retreats and every class he taught to try to wrap my brain around this Spirituality thing.

Growing up, there was no Spirituality, and the God I had was very punishing. My parents taught me that, to make "It" happen, I should do more and achieve results. And later in life, I lived in a constant state of survival. However, Michael's philosophy was different. He said, "It's not about what you're trying to push yourself to achieve Kim, such as the house and white picket fence, it's about what is seeking to emerge through you. What does your soul desire?"

Every day, I would sit in meditation and ask myself, "What is seeking to emerge through me?" As I contemplated what my purpose was, many times the answer was vague. However, what did come were glimpses around the corner to my new life—a peek at what was to come. During my visioning, I would ask myself, "When I was happy and felt free, what was I doing?" I realized I was the most free and creative when I was a child. So, I asked myself, "What did I love to do when I was a child?" What I found was that I have always been doing what comes naturally to me. For example, I was counseling others. My earliest memory of counseling was when I was three, and I was trying to help my mom. In high school, they nominated me the school counselor. A recovery home hired me to help kids my age who had challenges with addiction. As a result, my high school asked me to enter competitions for writing and public speaking, and I won.

I also had a creative side. I was often alone, so my creative mind would invent new projects, like making lollipops and treats and then selling them door to door, or swimming at the local golf course lake to retrieve the flyaway balls and sell them back to the golfers. Nobody taught me how to do this. It was what I did naturally for fun. I realized that being an entrepreneur and teaching others about Mental Focus, Emotional Fitness, and Physical Training through Integrative Mentoring was my niche. And now I am going to help you find yours.

"I believe that you're great, that there's something magnificent about you. Regardless of what has happened to you in your life, regardless of how young or how old

you think you might be, the moment you begin to think
properly, this something that is within you, this power
within you that's greater than the world, it will begin
to emerge. It will take over your life. It will feed you, it
will clothe you, it will guide you, protect you, direct you,
sustain your very existence. If you let it! Now that is what
I know, for sure"
—Michael Bernard Beckwith

Now, if you already know what you want, great! Use your Hour of Power every morning to become clear on the direction you need to go, and vision it. Create a vision board, look at it, and visualize your success daily. If you are not clear on what you want, keep reading.

One suggestion would be to sit quietly and use your morning meditation to become clear. Remember: that first hour in the morning is gold. Use it wisely. I call it my Hour of Power. While you are sitting in meditation, ask yourself: What is seeking to emerge through me? Is it a better body, is it better health, better relationships? Do you want to create a new business? If so, what type? Many people say, "I don't know." My question to you is then, "What if you did know?" If you still can't come up with anything, then ask yourself, "What did I love to do when I was a kid? What could I spend hours and hours on and lose track of time doing it?" Did you love to play sports? If so, what type? Were they team sports? Solo sports? Contact sports? If you were on a team, more than likely, you would do well in a team environment at work. Or if you liked solo sports, or being an artist, maybe you are an introvert, and you like to work on your own. Whatever it is, write it down and incorporate it into your plan. If you do not see an image, do not worry. I would often leave my meditations with a feeling, and I would hold on to that feeling until ideas came into my mind that would match those feelings. Then I would write them down.

"When you visualize, then you materialize."
—Denis Waitley

Once you are clear on what is seeking to emerge through you, it's time to visualize. I remember working with my professional athletes. When they played a game, I would record them. Directly after the game, while their minds were still fresh, I would have them watch the video and identify what mistakes they had made. Once they told me, I asked them what the solutions were to those mistakes, and then we would discuss them. Together, we created a game plan around those solutions and visualized them succeeding. Most of those athletes didn't make the same mistakes twice because they planted the seeds in their unconscious minds of what they wanted, so the body followed.

"Your Goal and your Purpose are two different things.
Goals are what you want. Your purpose is what is seeking
to emerge through you."
—Kimberly Lou

Now that you know what is seeking to emerge through you, we can set goals. Goals naturally come when you are clear on your direction. And since you've made it through the mindset-training portion of your program, it's time to build a rocket ship to get you to the moon. In the following chapters, we will address goal setting and then help you create a daily plan of action, to guide you through your every-day-life with ease and grace.

CHAPTER XIII
The Purpose Behind Your Goal

"If you want to be happy, set a goal that commands your thoughts, liberates your energy and inspires your hopes."
—Andrew Carnegie

Goals: Getting Clear

Sometimes clients are hesitant about setting goals at the beginning of their program. "What's the use?" they say, "I have the very same goals as last year, and the year before that, and the year before that. The only difference is now, when I set goals, I feel like it's never going to happen." These beautiful beings are burned out from spinning their wheels going nowhere fast. Ask me how I know? This was my life for so many years. My intentions were true, and even though I could see in my mind what I wanted, I didn't have the tools to achieve it. I give myself an A for effort; however, that effort burned me out. Setting one more goal seemed like chasing water in the middle of the desert. Every time I thought I'd reached success, that success would disappear like a mirage. I was left feeling hopeless, as if no change existed for someone like me.

Today, any time my clients say to me, "Kim, I want to lose weight and change my life; can someone like me change?" I say, "Absolutely! But first, we need to set goals. What exactly do you want?" The common answer is, "I don't know. I haven't thought about that." And there's the problem. More often than not, there is no clear intention, just a vague pipedream. That being said, most of my clients don't have a problem setting their business goals, their family goals, even their contribution goals. However, when it comes to self-care, most do not have a clue what to do. They only know they want to feel better.

Why is being clear so important? The reason most goals fail is because the person setting the goal usually doesn't have a specific blueprint, plan, or tools to use to get there—wherever "there" is. It's important to become clear on WHAT you want, and even more specifically WHY you want it to make change happen. I believe that, if you do not have your goals or the "why" for your goals, you won't be able to build that blueprint or plan to achieve them. Harvard did a study on this. They found that if someone created a vision of what they wanted and had a goal, they were 35% more likely to achieve that goal. Better yet, when those same people had a goal and a written blueprint or plan, and visualized it, they were more apt to achieve and sustain their goal 95% of the time. I have achieved this for myself and for many clients with great success.

So, that's what we are going to do for you. In the remaining portion of this chapter, we are going to focus on:

> **Step 1—Goals**: Specifically, I am going to help you become clear on what you want.
>
> **Step 2—Purpose**: The Why or Purpose behind those goals, creating a vision and a purpose that will keep you motivated to take action and sustain that action.
>
> **Step 3—Obstacles**: Clearing the obstacles standing in your way. Often, we have certain Belief Systems which cause us to fail, so we need to first identify those triggers that take us out. Once we determine your triggers, I will help you create a plan of action to stop them.
>
> **Step 4—Solutions**: Finding solutions to those obstacles. By coming up with a game plan for facing obstacles, you have the tools to confront them head on

and change them. Plus, you cannot create a new life if you do not plant new seeds and tend to them daily.

Step 5—Mental Imagery: Every day, you will look over your goals, your whys, and your action plan, to plant new seeds of success in your unconscious mind. You will do this to point the brain in the right direction to reach your dreams and desires. You don't know how to live this new life yet. If you do not plant new seeds, you will revert back to old behaviors. Daily mental imagery will point your brain in the right direction towards success.

"If the ladder is not leaning against the right wall, every step we take just gets us to the wrong place faster.
—Steven Covey

The main idea when Goal Setting is that we need to know what we want, but we also need to create a mindset shift. We are learning to create a blueprint for living. Many coaches would have you set your goals in the beginning of their program. However, Steven Covey says, "It's great to set goals, but make sure your ladder is leaning against the right wall." Your *Becoming Who You're Meant to Be* program is that wall, and it's going to determine whether you will be able to sustain your journey and ensure you have the energy to achieve your goals.

First, let me help you get clear on your goals and the reasons why you want your goals to happen. *Your WHY needs to be so important that, if the only time you have to work out is 5 a.m., you will do it!* So, grab a pen and a piece of paper, and let's get started!

System for Goal Setting

As we begin, make sure you turn off your cell phones or anything that dings or distracts you. We are going to identify what kind of lifestyle it would take for you to become Emotionally Fit. There are three main areas to help: Mental Goals; Physical Goals; and Emotional/Spiritual Goals.

Area #1—Mental Goals: Are you emotionally stable, or do you stress easily? Do you feel like you get to play, or are you in survival mode all of the time? How would you like to feel? Would you like to become stress free? Would you like to become more confident? Whatever you want to start feeling, write it down. Often, it's our relationships that take us out of the game of life. Sometimes there are people we need to let go of. Sometimes we need to set boundaries. Often, we can't even begin to have relationships with other people until we heal the main relationship—the one with ourselves. That being said, how do you want to treat yourself? How do you want to talk to yourself? Some say that the way we treat ourselves far outweighs the abuse that we may take from others. Ask yourself what kind of relationship you want with others, and make sure you have the same kind of relationship with yourself. Write it down.

Area #2—Physical Goals: You may say you want to lose weight, but what does that mean? How much weight do you want to lose? In what amount of time do you want to lose it? Be realistic; losing 10 lbs. in a week will not usually work. A healthy amount would be 1 ½ - 2 lbs. Do you want to be lean and skinny? Or do you have a thicker frame that puts on more muscle? Or maybe it's none of those, and you simply want to be more vibrant and have more energy. Be specific. It sounds simple, but people often think, "Well, maybe I'm not allowed to have what I want. Is it even possible to have what I want?" For now, I want you to daydream. In a perfect world, what would feel good to you and your body type? Write it down.

Area #3—Emotional/Spiritual Goals: What are your spiritual goals? Do you want to become more connected to your Creator? Do you want to learn to meditate? To visualize? What time of the day would you like to meditate? Would you like to read more motivational or spirituality-based books? Would you like to attend church on Sundays? Tithe more? Whatever your Spiritual Goals are, write them down.

> *"If you don't design your own life plan, chances are you'll fall into someone else's plan. And guess what they have planned for you? Not much."*
>
> —Jim Rohn

Now you have your goals. It's important to put them into a time frame for when you will accomplish them.

Taylor.

I was working with Taylor, a student, and I asked him to write his plan. He kept putting it off and putting it off, and then he put it off some more.

Finally, I said, "What are you doing right now?"

He said, "Nothing."

"Wonderful!" I said. "Get a piece of paper. Let's write a plan."

We sat there for an hour, wrote down his goals and his time line and put together a plan. Something magical happened when he put a date next to his goals. They started to get done quickly because he had a road map. Not only that, many other amazing achievements started to happen in every area of his life. However, there was a reason he had been procrastinating: at an unconscious level, he knew he would need to step up his game. He couldn't hide behind his procrastination or perfectionism any more. (By the way, perfectionism equals procrastination.)

When you set a goal, make sure you want what you say you want and start with the end in mind. Let's do that now.

Part 1: Write down your long-term vision of what you want in each of the three areas. For example, in my physical area, I want to lose 20 lbs. and feel healthy and vibrant. What I need to do is:

1. Create an exercise plan
2. Create a food plan
3. Create a self-care plan

Part 2: Break each of these steps down into smaller bite-sized chunks; what are your goals for the week? For example:

Exercise:
- I will exercise five times this week
- I will use weights three times per week and perform cardio twice per week
- Monday, I will work Back and Biceps; Wednesday, Legs; Friday, Chest and Triceps; Tuesday and Thursday, mild cardio for 25 minutes.

Nutrition:
- Eat three meals a day and two snacks
- Create a meal plan that works for my body
- Write a grocery list
- Go grocery shopping on Sunday
- Prepare foods on Sunday and Wednesday

Self-Care:
- Create a morning routine: Wake up - Read - Write - Meditate
- Create a bedtime routine: Bed Time - Read - Write - Meditate

Part 3: Then make it even more specific. What do you need to do today in order to achieve your goal?

Exercise:
- Myofascial release - 5 Minutes
- Reconstructive exercise - 5 Minutes
- Workout with weights - 35 Minutes
- Stretch - 5 Minutes
- If my body is okay, 20-30 minutes of cardio after workout

Nutrition:
- Breakfast – Egg white omelet
- Lunch – Tuna with yams
- Snack – Handful of almonds
- Dinner – Salmon with a veggie
- Snack – 2 oz. of Turkey and 1 tablespoon of avocado

Self-Care:
- Wake up: Read - Write - Meditate - 15 Minutes
- Bedtime: Turn off electronics one hour before bedtime; take a hot shower or bath; Read - Write - Meditate - 15 Minutes

There is your goal-setting portion. When you break down goals from the big picture to a daily routine, it helps you get clear on the daily action you need to take, and it takes away the pressure of having to get it all done now.

I remember telling a friend, "This project is so big, how am I going to get it all done?"

He said to me, "How do you eat an elephant?"

"I'm not sure... How?" I said.

He said, "One small bite at a time."

I never forgot that. By creating small sustainable steps (I call this chunking), I was able to complete the project without all of the stress. When I implemented structure, I didn't waste time wondering what I had to do next. I simply had to look at my plan and do the next indicated step.

In the next chapter, we will become even clearer on setting up your plan and on adding that daily plan into your lifestyle. Now, we will address our Why's.

What is the Why behind your goal or better yet your purpose?

Your Why is the most important part of your program. Although this program is simple, it is not easy. There will be days when you want to quit. Your Why is going to get you through it. I know this to be true for my clients and for myself. At first, I was all gung-ho to make a change, but then something happened. Life got in the way. My body and mind retaliated. I was met with major resistance, and I reverted right back to my old behaviors. Every day, I would start again, and every day I would fail. I called this "failing forward." However, when I became clear on the Why behind my desire to change—which was so I could to be around to take care of my daughter, sustain my big lifestyle, and have the energy to do it all—it catapulted my success. At last, I was able to push through to the other side of the resistance.

Now, how do we find our Why? We have to go to your past, your bad habits, and everything you don't like about yourself to discover the gem in it. Your Why is hiding in there. Remember the story of my client in Chapter Three who told me he wanted to be big and strong because "the chicks dig it"? When I asked him why it was important for the chicks to dig it, he said, "Because I don't want to be manipulated or domi-nated." When I said, "Is that what is happening to you now?" he was amazed that I could make that connection. What we resist, persists. When you are resisting or avoiding a painful experience, especially from your past, that is exactly what you will attract. By thinking that he didn't want to be manipulated or dominated, my client was drawing in exactly that. His Why for being big and strong needed to be bigger and stronger than that negative thought.

Remember the chapter on the Universal Language of Energy? Whatever energy you're carrying is what you will attract. It's kind of like a salesman who, deep inside, thinks he can't sell. Even if he says he can with his words, his body language is saying something entirely different. It's called a self-fulfilling prophecy, and I see this all the time. How do we solve it? We have to focus on the opposite of that.

Peter.

I said to Peter, my client, "What is the opposite of being manipulated and dominated?"

He said, "I want to be healthy so that I can attract healthy relationships into my space."

I said, "What a wonderful goal. That, I can get on board with."

Then I asked him, "How does that feel when you say that?"

He said, "I feel free!"

"That's exactly how it should feel. Free! Now, would you say that your WHY is to feel healthy enough to attract healthy people?"

"Yes, that's exactly it."

I said, "Write that down and look at it every day."

So, what is your Why? Make it super important. Eliminate the goals that don't align with it, and write it down.

Clearing Obstacles

"Obstacles don't have to stop you. If you run into a wall, don't turn around and give up. Figure out how to climb it, go through it, or work around it."
—Michael Jordan

Now we are going to talk about obstacles. Oh, there will be obstacles, and usually the obstacles standing in the way are you and your thoughts. "Why?" you may ask. Most of us are only 5% conscious. The other 95% is unconscious. That 95% beats my heart, breathes my lungs, and allows me to drive my car, drink my tea, reach back and wipe my kid's nose, and arrive at school 20 minutes later, not knowing how I got there. That same unconscious is very upset if you change on him/her. When one begins a new program, the 95% will battle the 5%, and who do you think is going to win at first, just by sheer numbers? That is why most of the time when you start a new program, you will quit. The cavalry will outnumber you. So, you need to create an offensive plan to ensure, when obstacles come up, you know how to eliminate them immediately.

Some people say, "I don't know what my obstacles are, Kim." I say, not to worry. Look at the obstacles that have stood in your way in the past. Do you see a common behavior that has seemed to limit you? Usually it's a trigger, and those triggers can take you out quickly! So, the trick is to find those triggers before you start this program, so when they come up, you will have the solution in your tool belt.

The moral of the story is that there are always going to be obstacles standing in your way. Obstacles can take many forms and none of us are immune. Here's a little bit about what happened to me. I developed a condition where, no matter what I ate, my body would have major pain. Even when I drank water. After over $30,000 worth of CT scans, ultra sounds, MRI's and then therapy, the doctors all told me I was crazy and this condition was all in my head. I was not only in major pain, I felt guilt and shame and made myself wrong for having it! And part of the diagnosis was right. I was super, duper stressed-out from all of life's demands such as running my own business and being a single parent. I didn't have the tools to be able to take care of myself. Because of the major amount of self-inflicted stress, and by not taking care of myself, my body retaliated. I was in so much pain I became an irritable mother and a burned-out coach who was not following my own advice!

My story is not unusual. That is life. It's the challenges that help us grow and turn out to make life interesting and fun. Remember: there is always a solution for every obstacle. So, what are the obstacles standing in your way? Boredom? Not enough time? Lack of planning? Lack of support? Whatever comes up, write it down on the left side of a piece of paper. In a moment, we will write down solutions to those obstacles on the right side of that paper.

Solutions for Clearing Obstacles:

There are going to be times when you want to reach for that piece of candy, or not wake up to do your exercise. It is important to create solutions, so when you are in an intense state, you automatically go into your tool box, pick the tools you need, and achieve your results and goals.

The way to create sustainable results is to tackle the small obstacles first. We will learn to "eat the elephant" one bite at a time as we take small consistent steps towards your goals. What if one of your obstacles is that you have a hard time staying out of the freezer for a midnight ice cream snack? What is your solution to that? If you do not have the support you need, who can you call and ask for help? When you know you won't show up to work out at the gym, who can you call to meet you there? Whatever your solution is, write it down on the right side of your obstacle list. Look at it every day. Think of possible solutions for all the obstacles on your list. Write them down.

Visualize How Your Life Would Be If You Were Living the Solutions:

To change a physical or mental limitation, you must first change it in your mind. Once those limitations are addressed, the results will come because you will be taking right action. Unfortunately, most people do not believe change can happen for them. They think it's for everyone else. However, when a person believes he can do anything, he acts on it and obtains a result. The only difference between people who are successful and those who are not is that those who are successful faced their fears and took appropriate action. No matter what. Those who didn't stayed stuck on a hamster wheel, spinning their wheels going nowhere fast. That's why we need to get into a daily state of awareness. Each day when you wake up, look at your goals, read or watch an inspirational YouTube video, and visualize your day.

As for me, every morning I ask myself two main questions: "How am I going to condition my mind for success today and get myself into a peak state to act?" And, "How can I change my mindset and act on a skill today to create freedom in my life?" Then, I sit quietly and wait for the answer and write it down. Once I have written it down, I visualize acting on that. If I can't come up with a clear vision, I write down what I want to have happen and then read it aloud. I swear this works every time.

My Promise To You!

My promise to you is that if you follow this program you will heal and restore your health and energy, and you'll become more vibrant. You will fall in love with life again. If weight loss is what you want, you will do that, too. If you look at your goals, your Whys, your obstacles, your solutions, and visualize success every day—then act on your goals—you will succeed. That is my promise to you.

Now that we've talked about goal setting, let's show you how to add your busy life into your self-care plan.

CHAPTER XIV
Planning versus Structure

"By failing to prepare, you are preparing to fail."
—Benjamin Franklin

Let's talk about preparation and planning to help you create a sustainable structure and thereby assist you in managing your energy. If you are anything like me, when someone mentions the word "structure," you may want to cringe. It's almost as if there were a noose around your neck, and my clients are no different. If you don't have a structure, or if you have a hard time implementing one, you may have had either too much structure or not enough when you were a child. It's that mindset of, "Don't tell me what to do!" Chances are, if you are reading this and you have that kind of mindset, you are probably your own boss or a very difficult employee to manage.

As a result, this is one of the most challenging portions of this program because most people are set in their ways and do not want to change. They may say they do; however, the evidence is clear. Most structure, even though it is necessary, doesn't sit well with my Type A personalities. However, in order to create the life they love, they need to develop a plan of action so it frees them up from whatever is draining their energy. That is what we will do for you. To begin, we must rearrange your mindset about what structure means. For example, in the past, you may have experienced someone such as a parent or authority figure who implemented structure or didn't provide enough. What that may have meant to you was the structure either wasn't safe and might easily collapse, or it was too confining. That may have left you feeling like you were walking on eggshells, or like you were stuck and could never change.

Caitlin.

Caitlin was a client who was addicted to drugs and had been in and out of treatment centers.

She looked at me with crocodile tears in her eyes and said, "Can someone like me ever change?"

I said, "Absolutely. The only difference between you and me is that I have tools and you don't. You are not broken; you are just at a breaking point. And right before a breakthrough, there is a break down. That's where you are right now—the breakdown."

She had been abused as a child and trusted no one. To her, creating and implementing a plan of structure meant feeling vulnerable, unsafe, and ultimately out of control. However, with my help and her willingness to change her mindset, she could finally surrender to the idea and create a new, more positive way of looking at change as something freeing. But she still needed to roll up her sleeves and do the work. With my help and her determination, she was able to get sober and change her life forever.

My philosophy of structure is something that will free up your time and energy. I'll illustrate with another story.

Jessica.

I was talking to Jessica the other day, and we were going over her plan and discussing her daily life. She was tolerant of me at first. However, I could clearly see in her face and hear in the tone of her voice that she was annoyed with me and resistant to my questions.

I kept probing her, asking, "Okay, tell me what your morning is like. When do you wake up? When do you eat? What do you eat? Now, tell me what your afternoon is like." I kept drilling and drilling.

She even said, "I don't want to go there! I don't want to talk about this anymore."

I then said, "I hear you, yet we need to keep going. Now, what time to you drive to work? When do you come home from work?"

Begrudgingly, she answered all of my questions, but I could tell she was still very annoyed. At the end of our session, I thanked her for being so cooperative, and she left. I chuckled to myself because I knew what I was doing, even though she didn't. You see, I know that the brain loves questions, and when you ask your brain the right questions, it will get to work in figuring out solutions for you. I knew that if I kept asking her questions and encouraging her to answer them, even if her answers were half-hearted, it would open the way for new seeds to be planted.

A couple of days later, she came to me and said, "Oh my gosh! Kim, thank you so much! I am so happy because what I realized is by creating that plan and removing the blocks to planning and structure, it freed up my schedule. I am saving two hours of drive time every day because I can work most days from home. Not only that, I don't have to hire the dog walker since I can do it myself. How cool is that?"

I knew she would have that breakthrough. I needed to break through to her unconscious mind—by asking her a bunch of annoying questions—for her to realize that on her own. This hasn't only worked in her life: I have seen this work in my life and in thousands of my clients' lives.

> *"Every minute you spend in planning saves 10 minutes in execution; this gives you a 1,000 percent return on energy!"*
> —Brian Tracy, author and motivational speaker

There is so much energy to open up and release when one has a structure or plan in place. Like Jessica, that's what I will help you see. It's that plan, that structure, which is the key to freeing up your life and schedule. How did I learn this? By watching nature. Nature is one of my best teachers. I love studying animals, especially wolves and how they live in the wild. When you're a wolf, basically every day you exercise whether you want to or not because you have to eat. Most wolves can walk up to ten hours every day when hunting for food. Even if they are not hungry, they hunt. Why? Because they keep that schedule which gives them a sense of structure. Every single wolf has a particular job or a purpose. There is a pack leader, there is a tail-end Charlie to protect the rear, there are wolves to the sides, and the elders' job is to stay with the cubs. The cubs' job is to play in order to learn new life skills. Every single one of those wolves has a purpose which then provides them with a sense of community and safety. It's all because of their structure.

On a side note, if you have ever seen a dog who doesn't get exercise, who doesn't have a structure or a purpose, you'll notice they develop neurotic behaviors. They chew the furniture or destroy the house. They can develop anxiety. They become aggressive and fixated on things. Some people might call those fixations addictions. Humans are no different. If we don't get the exercise we need—structure and a sense of purpose—we won't have a fulfilling life. In the past, I used to ask myself, "How can I fit my self-care plan into my busy life? How can I fit my workouts into my busy life? How can I fit my food plan into my busy life?" Now, my mindset is completely different. Now I ask myself, "How can I fit my busy schedule into my self-care plan? If I don't, it's never going to get done."

You see, here's the deal: if we do not add self-care into our daily lives, we will not sustain our big lives. We must make that self-care life plan a priority, so we can contain and sustain our big lives.

"Most of us spend too much time on what is urgent and not enough time on what is important."

—Stephen Covey

Let's begin to create that structure. We already know we need to read, write, and meditate. We also know we need to exercise and have a plan for nutrition. (For those of you who want to know more about nutrition, if you don't have my book, *Nutrition For Your New Age: Have Your Cake and Lose Weight, Too!,* you can purchase a copy on Amazon.)

A central feature of your new program is meal planning. This is important because there are certain times of the day when the body loves to eat. Additionally, our cortisol levels rise and fall at certain times of the day, so it is important to eat at those times because that will help you stay on track for your meals. This is vital to the success of your program. The first meal is breakfast and should be eaten between 7 - 8:00am in the morning. Ideally, lunch should be eaten between 11 - 12:00 noon. Next would be an afternoon snack between 2 - 3:30pm. The reason this is important is because cortisol levels take a big dive at about that time. There's a reason why many countries have *siestas* between 2:00 and 4:00pm in the afternoon. Most people are tired. I always tell CEO's or heads of big corporations that it's probably not a good idea to schedule board meetings at this time. Also, that's when most people reach for caffeine and sugary carbs because they are looking for quick energy. That's why it's super important to have a meal plan to keep you from crashing. Your next meal is preferably between 5 - 6:00pm. That's your dinner. The last meal of the day is between 9 - 10:00pm. (Frequently, my clients ask me, "Kim, why am I eating before bed?" It's really important, and I'll get to it in a minute.)

Next, you want to make sure you're having three meals and two snacks. I sing a song to help my daughter remember: "Breakfast, lunch, snack, dinner, snack. Breakfast, lunch, snack, dinner, snack." I sing it with a catchy tune that helps reinforce the mindset: "I've got to eat breakfast, lunch, snack, dinner and a snack."

What are the portions I want on my plate? If you are a woman, you would have:

Breakfast – Lunch – Dinner
- Protein – Fat – Carbs
- 3 to 4 oz of lean protein (any lean protein: turkey, chicken, fish, lean beef, tofu).
- 1 tbsp of fat (olive oil, peanut butter, avocado - you get the idea).
- 1/2 cup of low glycemic carbohydrates (brown rice, slow-cooked oatmeal, yams, etc.)

Snacks
- Afternoon Snack and Bedtime Snack
- These snacks consist of approximately 2 oz of protein and a fat.

If you feel the plan contains too much fat for you, then you can have green veggies instead (celery, kale, green beans, etc.). For those of you who don't like grains (personally, I can't eat them because they hurt my stomach), eat a piece of fruit like a peach or an apple.

If you are a man, you would have twice the amounts listed above. Let's add more meal plan details:

7 – 8am: Breakfast
- 3 to 4 oz of lean protein - 1 tbsp of fat - 1/2 cup of low glycemic carbohydrates or a piece of fruit.
- An example of a healthy breakfast might look something like three egg whites with one yolk, then 1/2 cup of cooked oatmeal. You can even add 1/4 cup of berries and some stevia to sweeten it.

11 - 12pm: Lunch

- 3 to 4 oz. of lean protein - 1tbsp of fat - 1/2 cup of low glycemic carbohydrates or a piece of fruit.
- A beautiful lunch would be 3-4 ounces of cooked salmon and a salad with every color of the rainbow in it. Get a little bit of greens, a little bit of shredded carrots (not too many carrots because the sugar content adds up), some red bell peppers, and maybe a couple of cherry tomatoes. Add a 1/2 yam, or if you prefer, cut up a medium size apple and put it in your salad. Now, add a couple of tablespoons of your favorite dressing and Voila! Lunch fit for a Queen or King!

2 – 3pm: Snack

- 2 oz. protein - 1 tbsp of fat
- What are some healthy snacks? Some people say 14 almonds. That doesn't do it for me. I need more than that. I like about twice that amount. Or, another idea could be 2 oz. of sliced turkey with 1/4 of an avocado. I'm not afraid of fats. Fats are an emulsifier, so it's important to eat them because they draw in the nutrients and vitamins that your brain and body need. Fats are also great for balancing hormones, especially in women, so don't feel the need to stay away from them; the right fat can be your friend. Healthy fats include olive oil and coconut oil. You can even try ghee butter from grass-fed cows.

5 – 6pm: Dinner

- 3 to 4 oz. of lean protein - 1 tbsp of fat - 1/2 cup of low glycemic carbohydrates or a piece of fruit.
- Dinner is very important, and it is the same formula as lunch. You can have chicken or steak. I

like steak. Some people say we shouldn't eat it. Again, steak is my friend, and at times, it's the only way I can stay on my food plan. That, along with some cooked spinach sautéed in 1/2 teaspoon of butter and 1/2 cup steamed rice will make a beautiful meal. If you're not having grains, add 1/2 of a sweet potato or yam, or you can take the carb out completely if you want to lose weight more quickly.

9 -10pm: Snack
- 2 oz. protein - 1 tbsp of fat
- The last meal of the day is a protein and a fat. One option is a protein shake with some peanut butter. If you don't like protein shakes, you can have a couple of slices of turkey and 1/4 avocado. Sometimes, I drink a protein shake with a little bit of peanut butter. You can also have a hard-boiled egg along with some salsa or vegetables.

Some of my clients question why they should eat a snack before bed. My answer is based on my having suffered from severe hypoglycemia years ago. I learned that, if I ate a little something before bed, it would balance out my blood sugar and reduce my hunger pangs throughout the night and into the next day. It also created a balance in my moods. You'll also have a better night's sleep, which is super important. Keep in mind, though, that you definitely do not want to have sugar before bed because it will spike your insulin levels and may interfere with your sleep.

* * * * *

So, there you have it! You don't want to try to fit your self-care plan into your busy life. You want to fit your busy life into that self-care plan. The first thing to do in the morning is read, write, and meditate. Then, make sure you have your breakfast, lunch, snack, dinner, and snack times planned and food prepared ahead of time. If you can't eat at those allotted times, I get it. But do what you can, and find time to eat three meals and two snacks in the day.

Next, write down your exercise times for each day. I usually do my reconstructive exercises and lift weights on Monday, Wednesday, and Friday, then fit in my reconstructive exercises and cardio on Tuesday and Thursday. If you decide you only want to work out three days a week, that's okay, too. It is still effective and better than nothing.

So, there's your schedule. If you want a free PDF Chart, head to my website and download it there at KimberlyLou. com. I've written it for you so you don't have to. Have fun with it. That schedule will free up your time so you can focus on the things that you love to do, whether that's being with your kids, or working, or enjoying life in general.

Don't worry. You don't have to do this alone. You can email me if you have questions or if you become confused in any way. Also, I have included tutorials and videos to guide you throughout this process. Once again, let me remind you that I'm here for you so you don't have to do this alone. We're going to work it out together!

Here is a suggested self-care structure for your day:

6:00am: Wake Up
- Read 5 Minutes
- Write 5 Minutes
- Meditate 5 Minutes

6:30am: Workout
- Myofascial release
- Reconstructive Exercises

- Workout
- Stretch
- Or Cardio or both on the days you have energy to do both

Meal Times

- 7:00 - 8:00 AM - Breakfast
- 11:00 - 12:00 PM – Lunch
- 2:00 - 3:00 PM - Snack
- 5:00 - 6:00 PM - Dinner
- 9:00 - 10:00 PM - Snack

10:00pm: Bedtime

- Read 5 Minutes
- Write 5 Minutes
- Meditate 5 Minutes

This Is Just the Beginning....Your New Adventure Awaits!

So, there you have it! We have discussed your old, limiting belief systems and how to unpack them, and we have given you the tools to rebuild and claim your new life. Remember, it takes 40 days to change a habit and 90 days to set it in stone and make it a lifestyle shift. Now that you know what to do, it's time to stand up and master your life to *Become Who You're Meant to Be.* When you do, watch how you will improve your performance and elevate yourself to the maximum levels of your ability.

And that isn't the end of your journey. Once you propel your life, your business, your mindset, and your body to supreme levels of success, my online resources and program will give you the tools you need in order to sustain your new amazing life. So, get ready for a new fun-filled, life-changing adventure.

I believe in you and I love you!

Kimberly Lou

ACKNOWLEDGMENTS

To Debra Waller who sat with me for hours to help me learn grammar and spelling. To my clients who allowed me to rant and rave about the ideas in this book. And allowed me to use their stories to help other people grow. To Jodie Shull who taught me how to be more positive in my writing and who copyedited for me. Jodie, I will never forget you sitting with me at Peet's Coffee reading this book for more than 9 hours straight. To my dear friend, Jimmy Peterson who saw a bigger vison for me than I could ever imagine and just by his friendship alone helped me gain the mindset to grow my business more than 20 times my normal income—because you encouraged me to take risks no matter what. To Mark. Sometimes God just sends you angels to help grow. Mark, thank you for your countless hours and support. Words cannot express my gratitude that you would be willing to listen to my ideas and help me put them into my video series and courses, my website and this program. Your encouragement and support have blessed me in so many ways.

And last, but not least. To my daughter, Summer. You are my life, my love, my EVERYTHING! You have pushed me to grow and to keep my word, and mostly you have given me the inspiration to be the kind of person I want you to grow up to be. Everything I do is for you. I am eternally grateful for you.

BECOMING WHO YOU'RE MEANT TO BE

Why is it so much harder to make it through the day? Where did my energy go? Most importantly, how do I get it back? If you are asking yourself these questions, please know that you are not alone. Millions of people just like you are trying to figure out why they feel constrained and drained throughout the day

FALL IN LOVE with Yourself and Your Life Again.

Becoming Who You're Meant to Be will help you shift out of survival mode and live a more vital, healthy, and happy life. This is a whole new journey you are going to take and, guess what? You don't have to do it alone! We are going to work it out together! *Becoming Who You're Meant to Be* details my Hero's Journey to healing, as well as a step-by-step guide to help you do the same. It wasn't until I stopped trying to force myself to make HUGE changes all at once that I was able to develop new patterns. By adding simple, small steps, I replaced my negative habits with healthy positive changes one little step at a time.

My promise to you is if you do what is suggested in *Becoming Who You're Meant to Be*, you will become more vibrant, you will learn to harness your energy, and you will find your motivation. *Becoming Who You're Meant to Be* will help you restore your health, as well as become more mentally, emotionally, and physically fit. *Becoming Who You're Meant to Be* will teach you how to lighten up and smile more while rolling with the punches of your fast-paced lifestyle. I have done all the research for you and have successfully trained over 10,000 people in my new methodology of Accelerated Performance ™ with sustainable results!

That pretty much sums up my whole approach to your new life, slow down to go fast. It doesn't matter whether it's your mental, emotional or physical wellbeing, it's all connected. So, let's shift from "settle and survive" into "accelerate and thrive," and into a life we love.

I love you,
Kimberly Lou.

Made in the USA
Lexington, KY
15 November 2019

57088539R00103